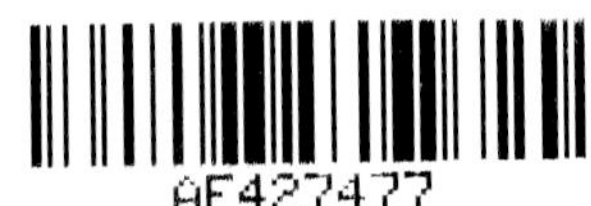

Serene Spirals

A Mandala Coloring Journey

Creative Quill Press

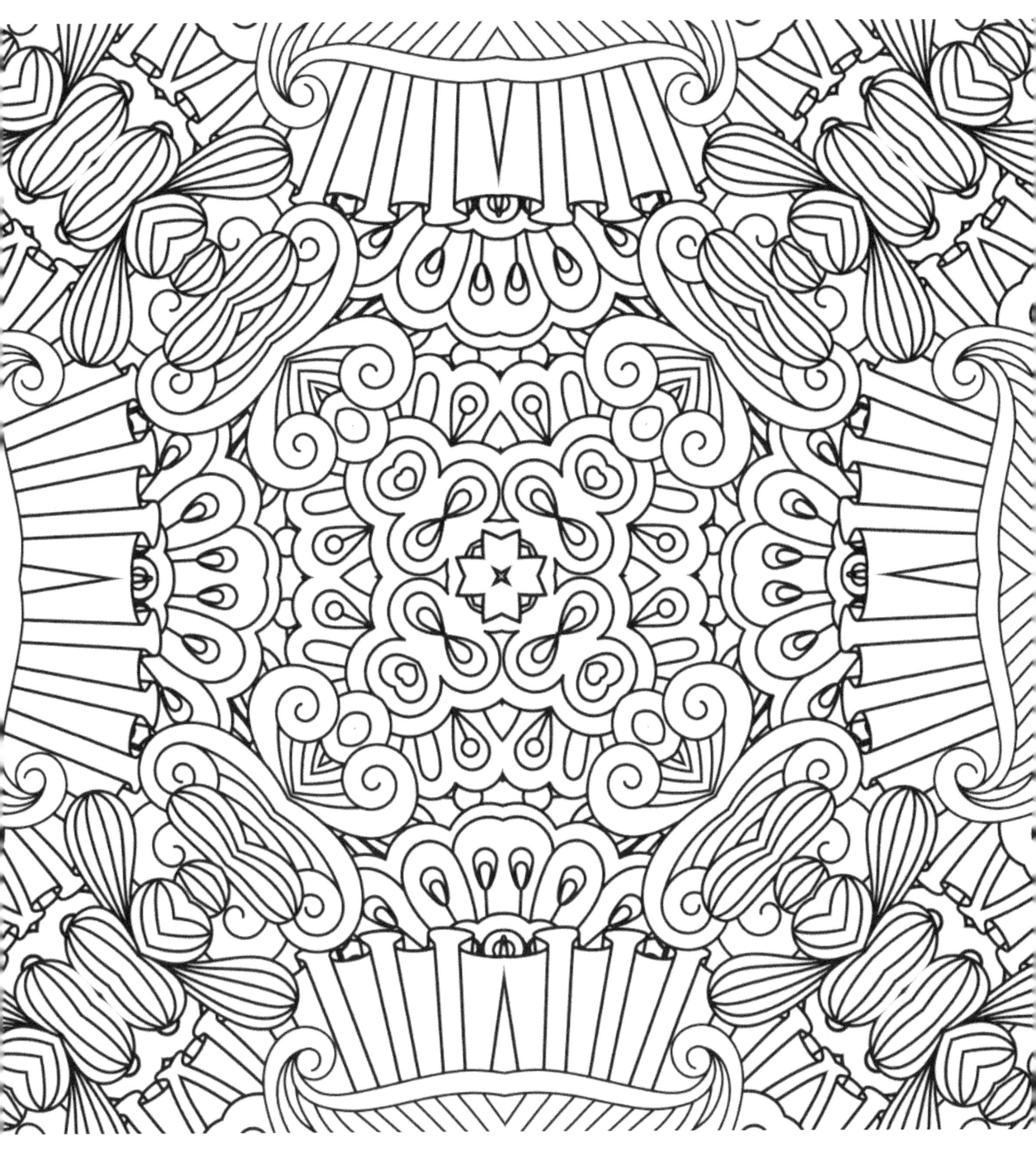

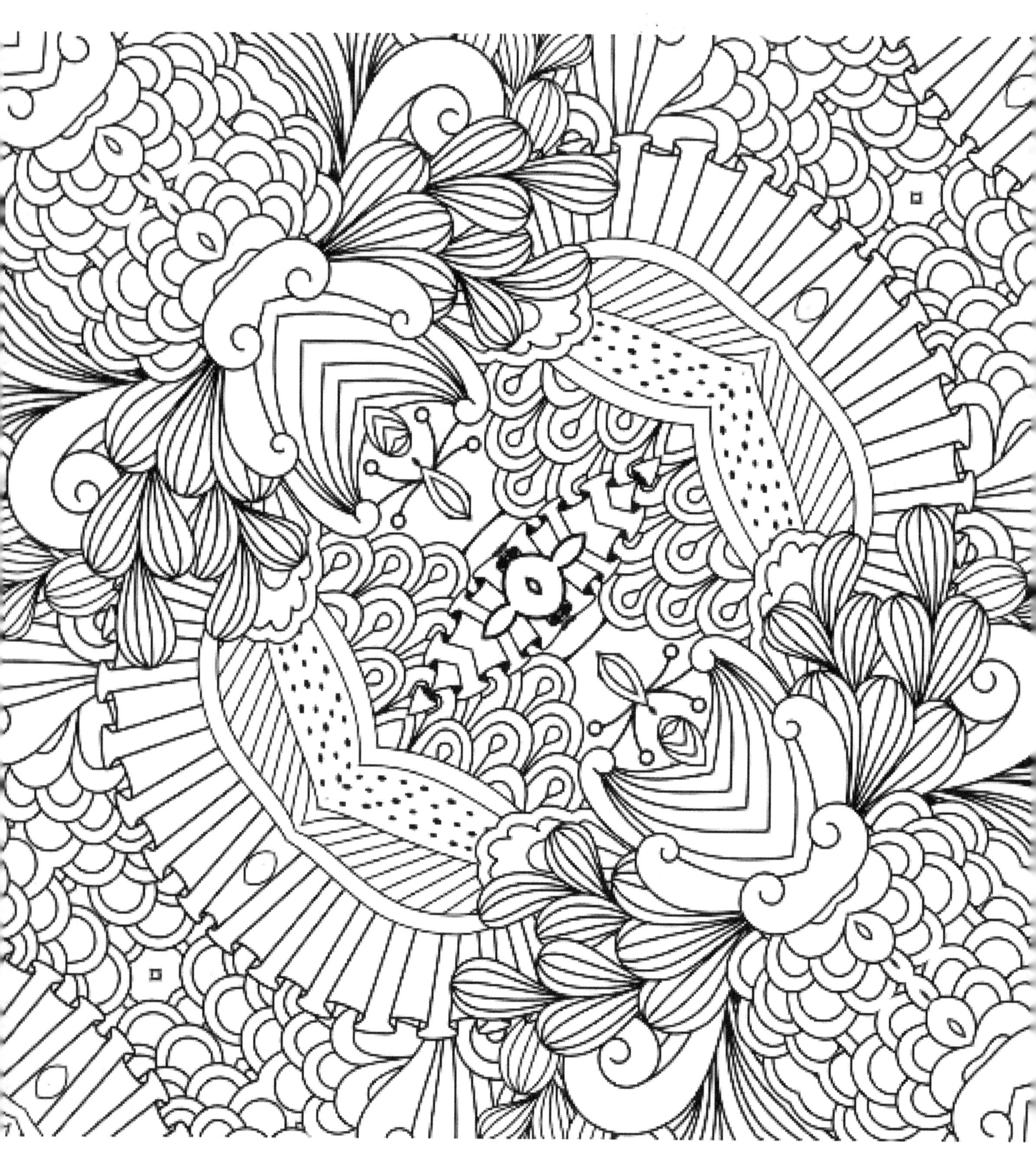

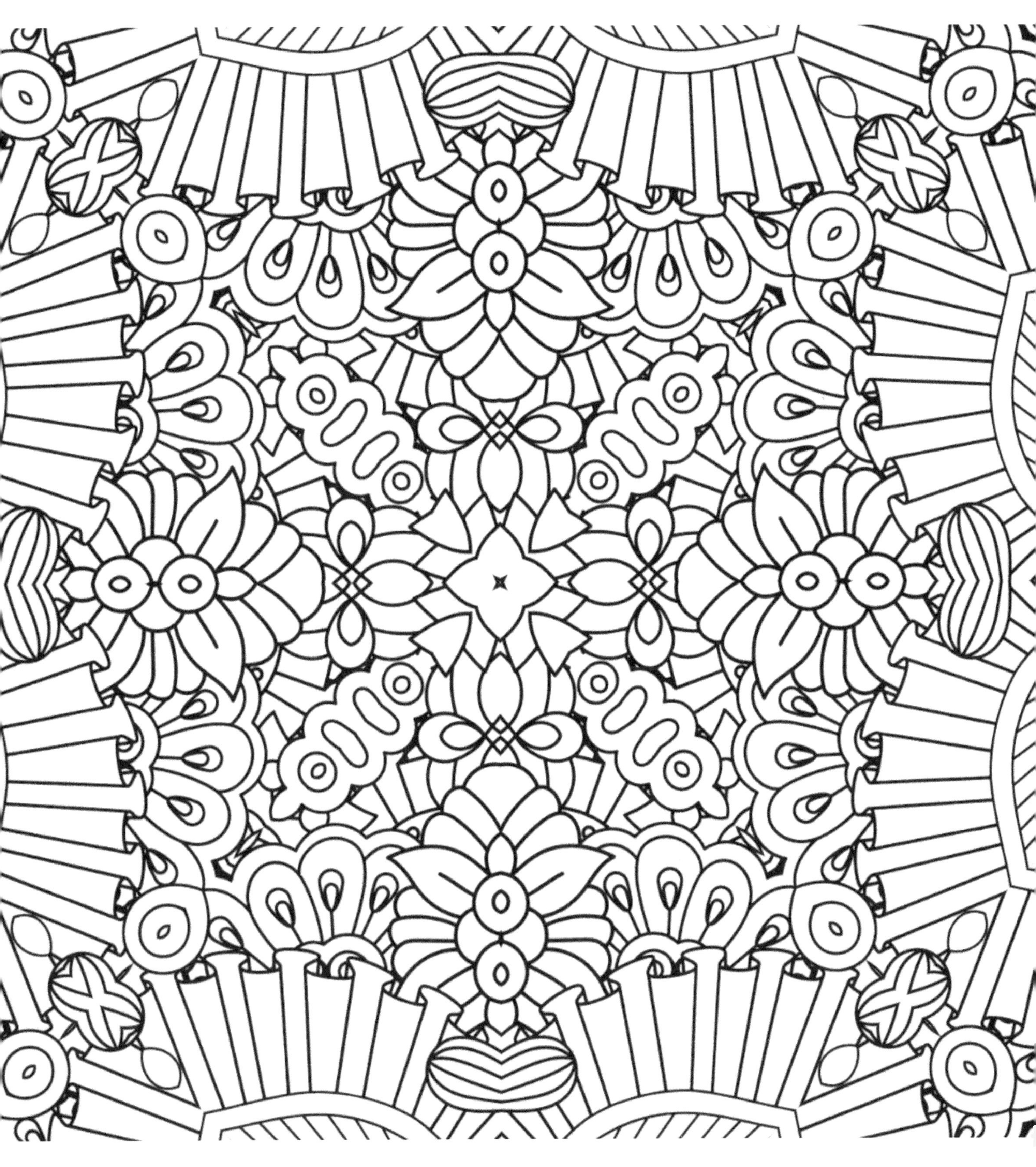

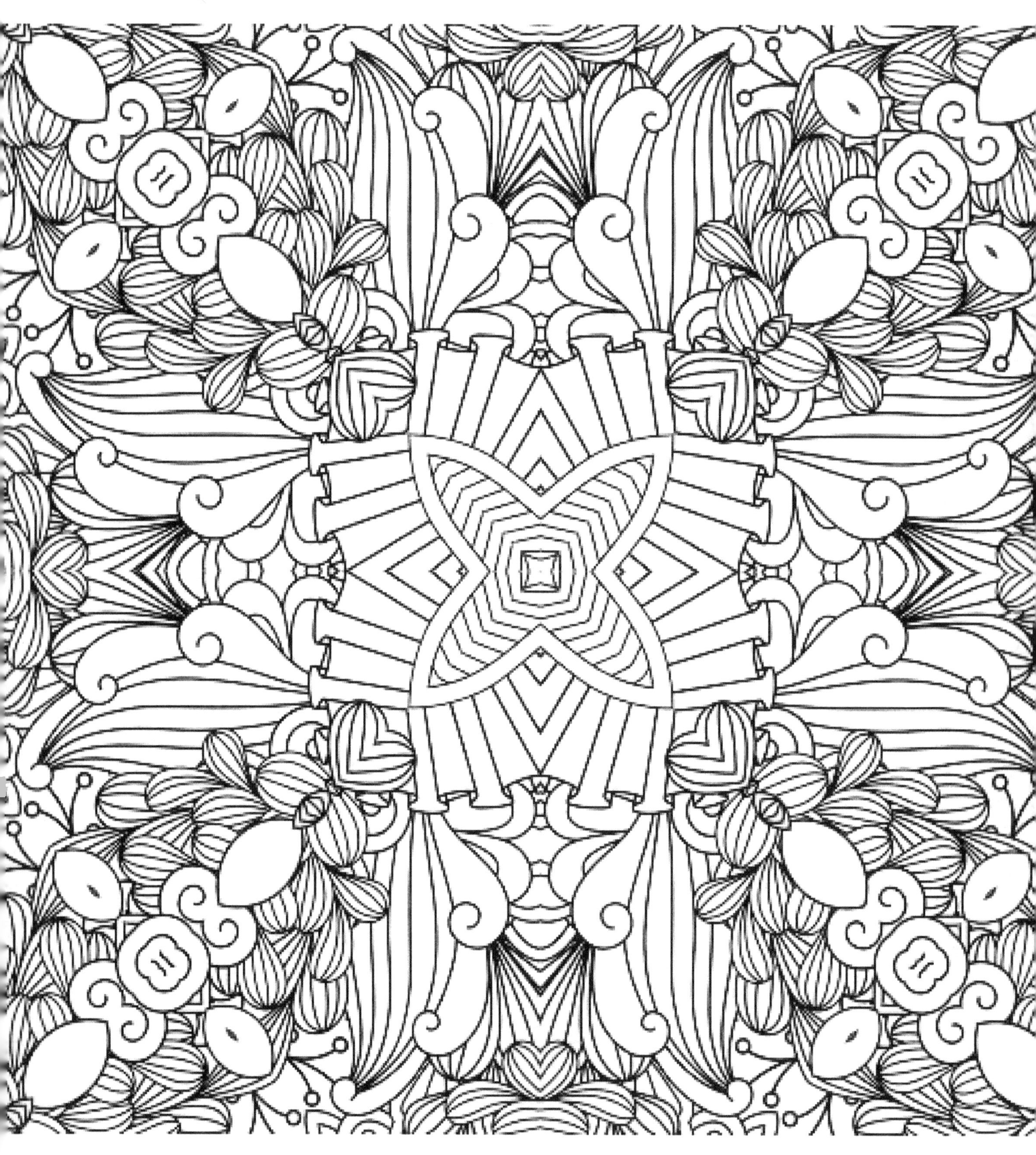

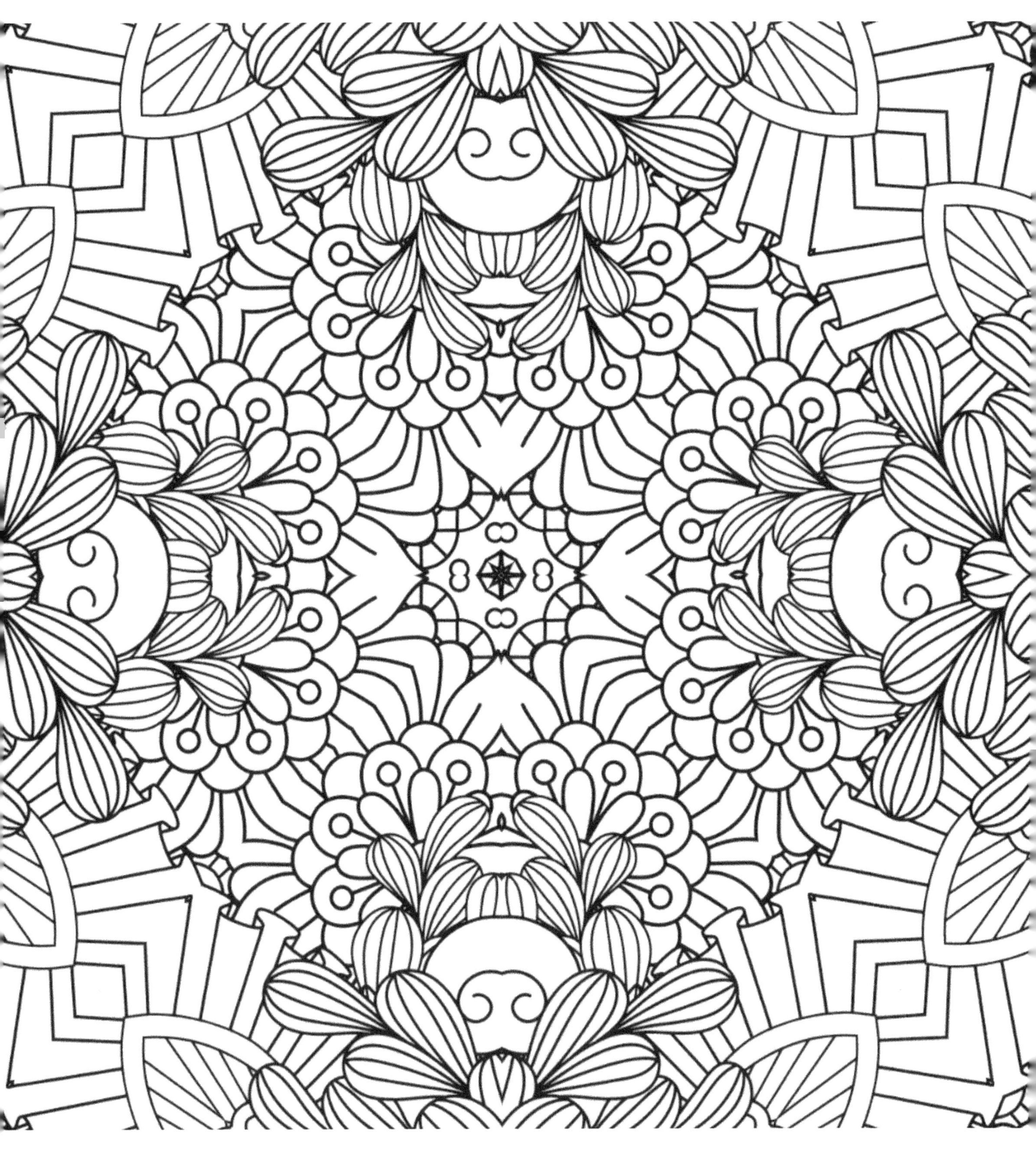

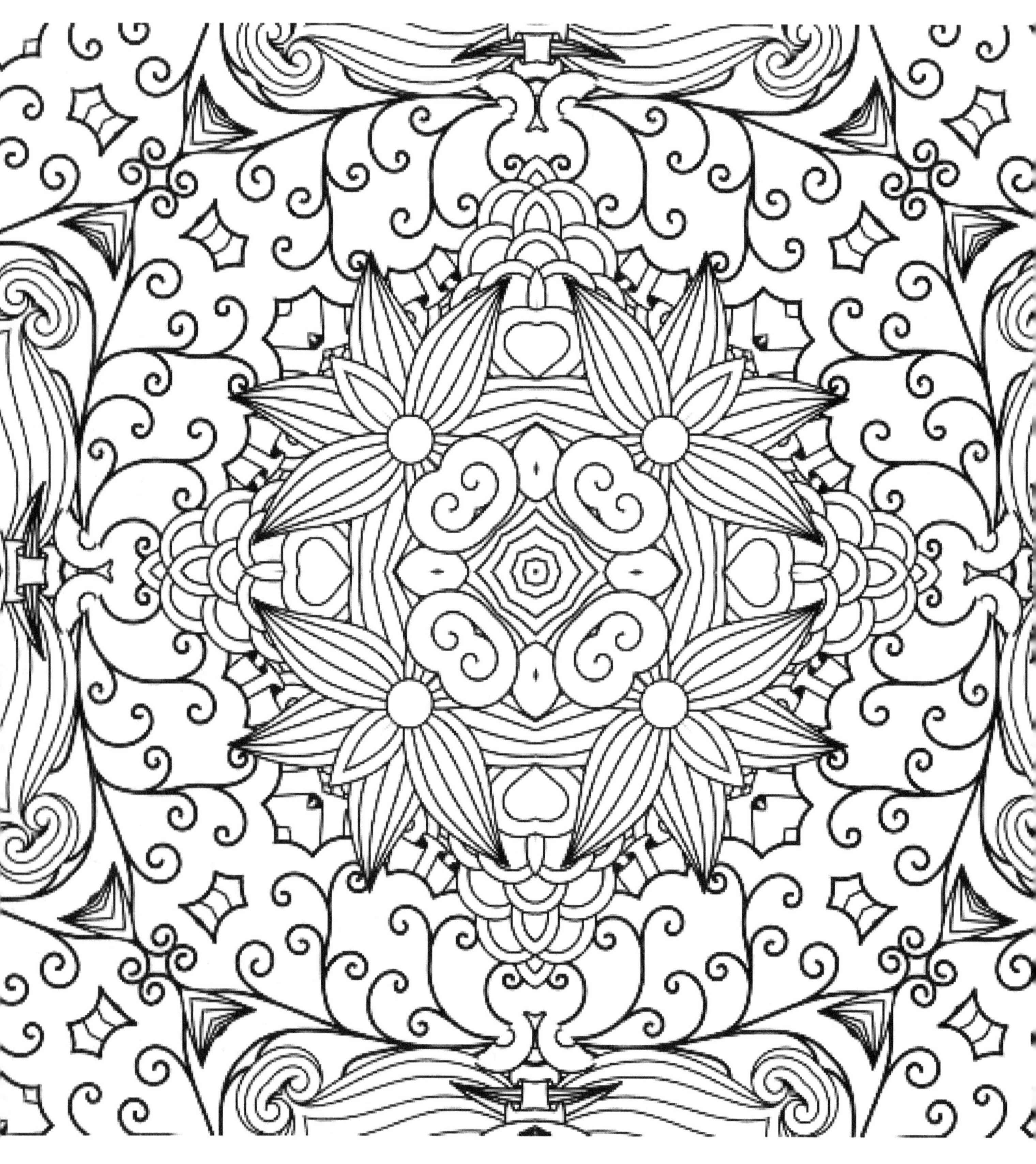

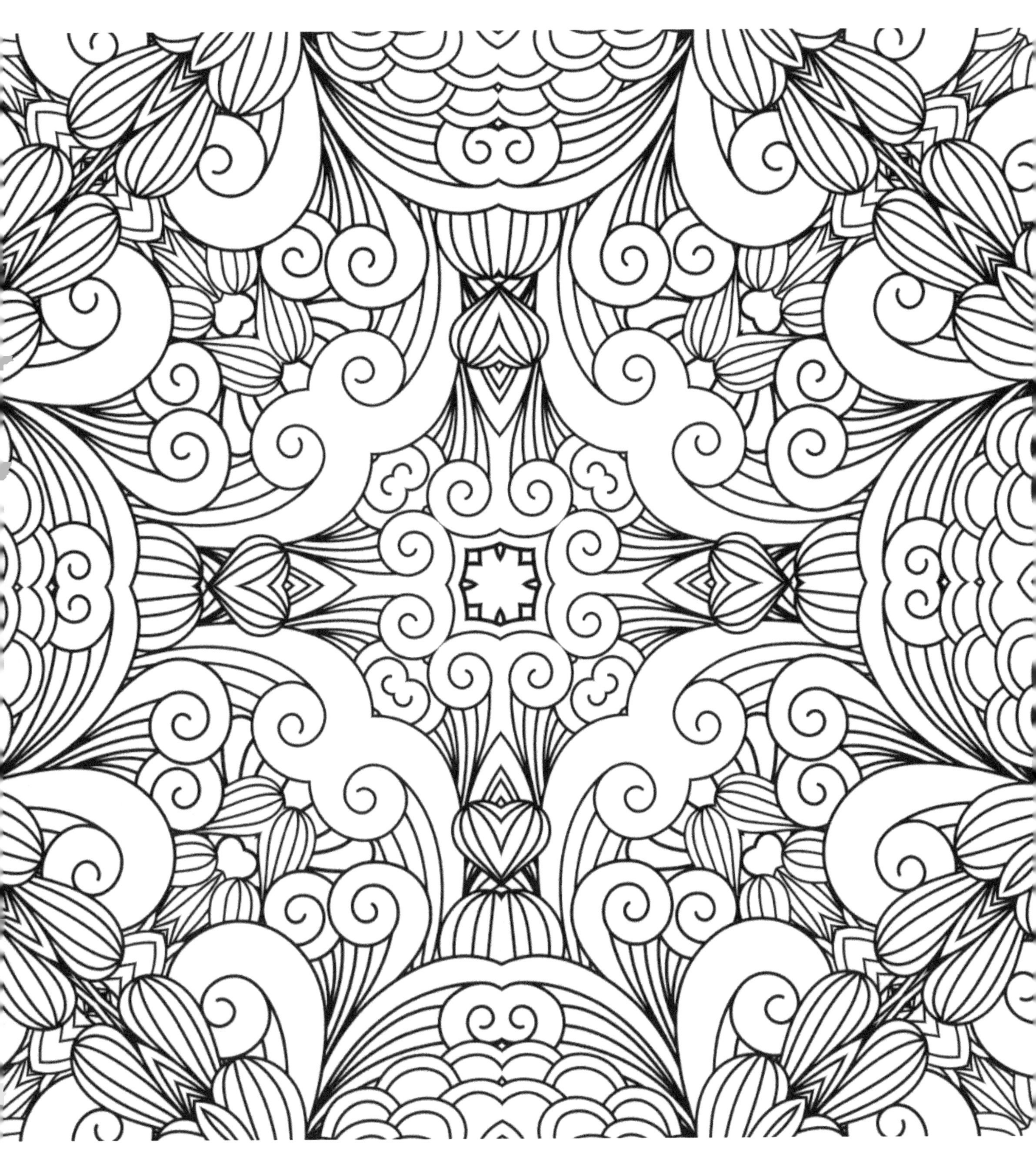

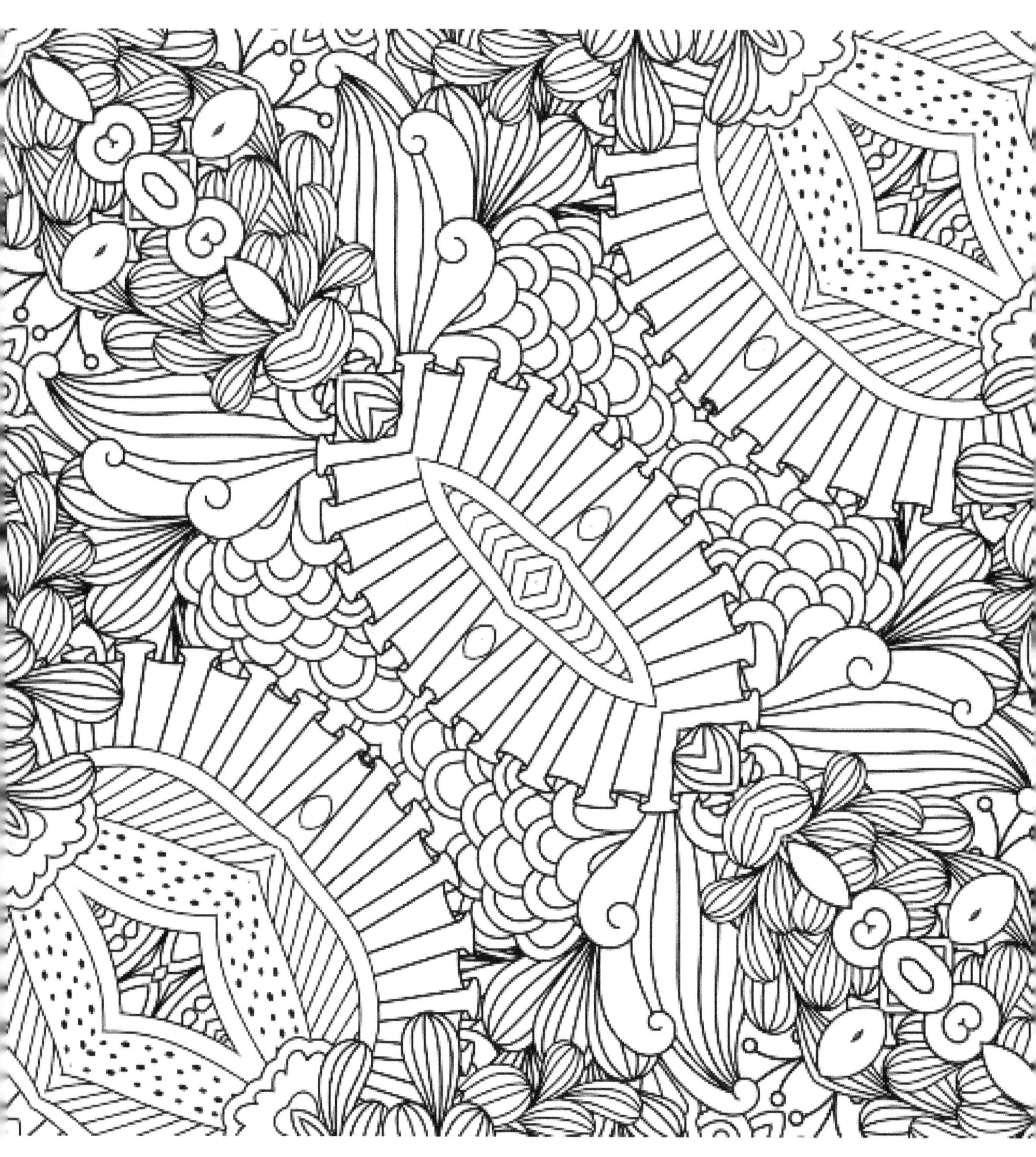

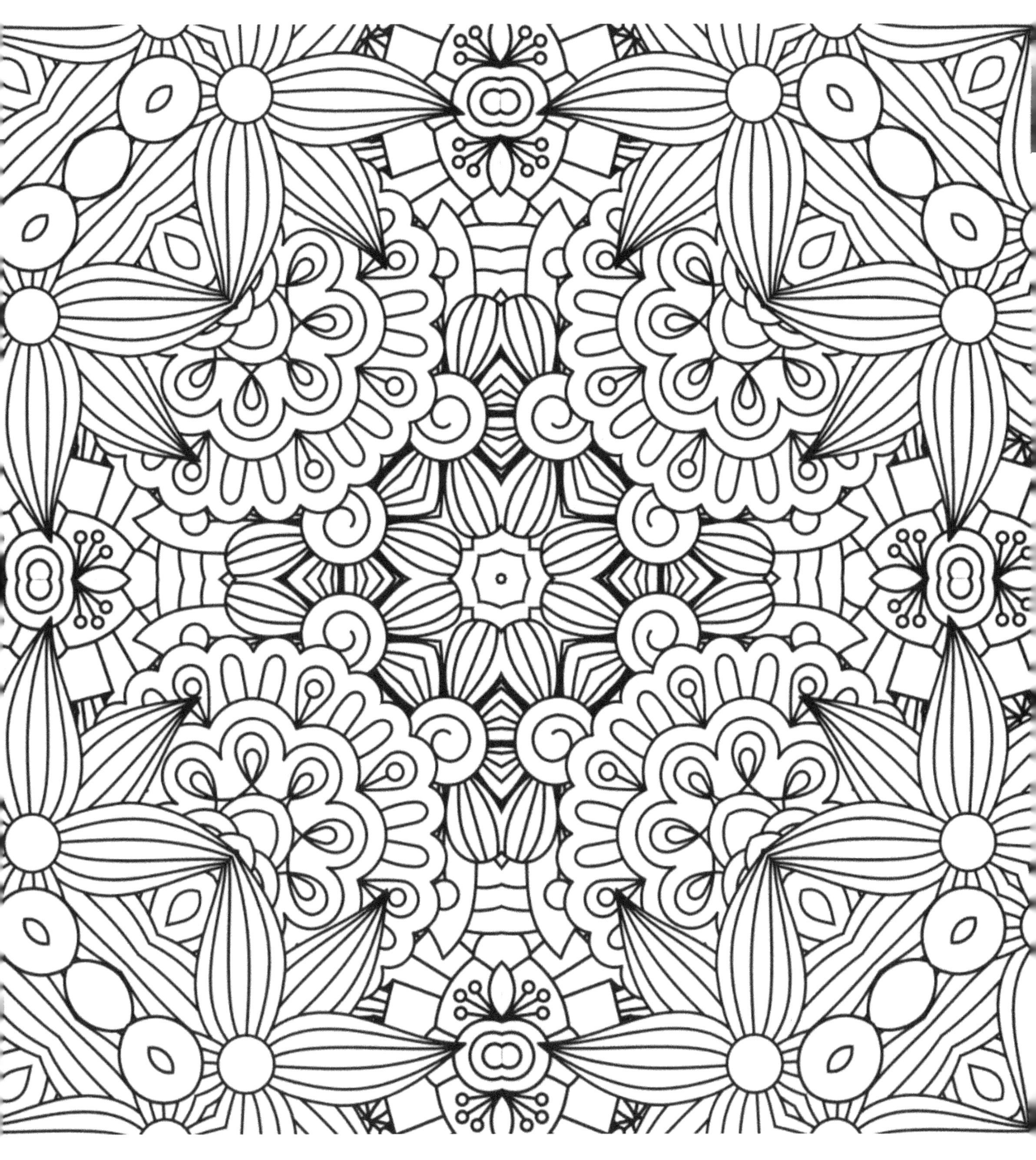

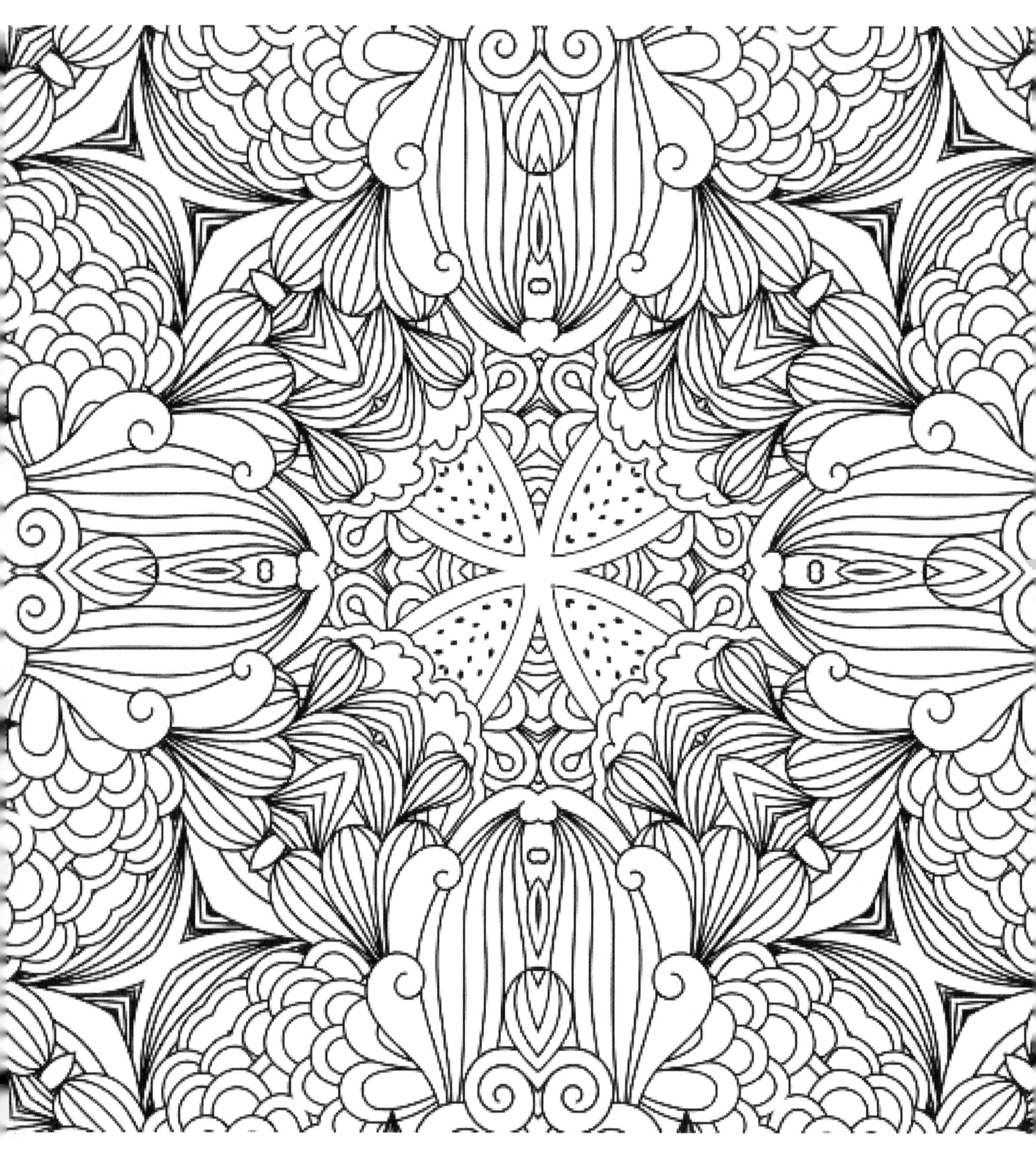

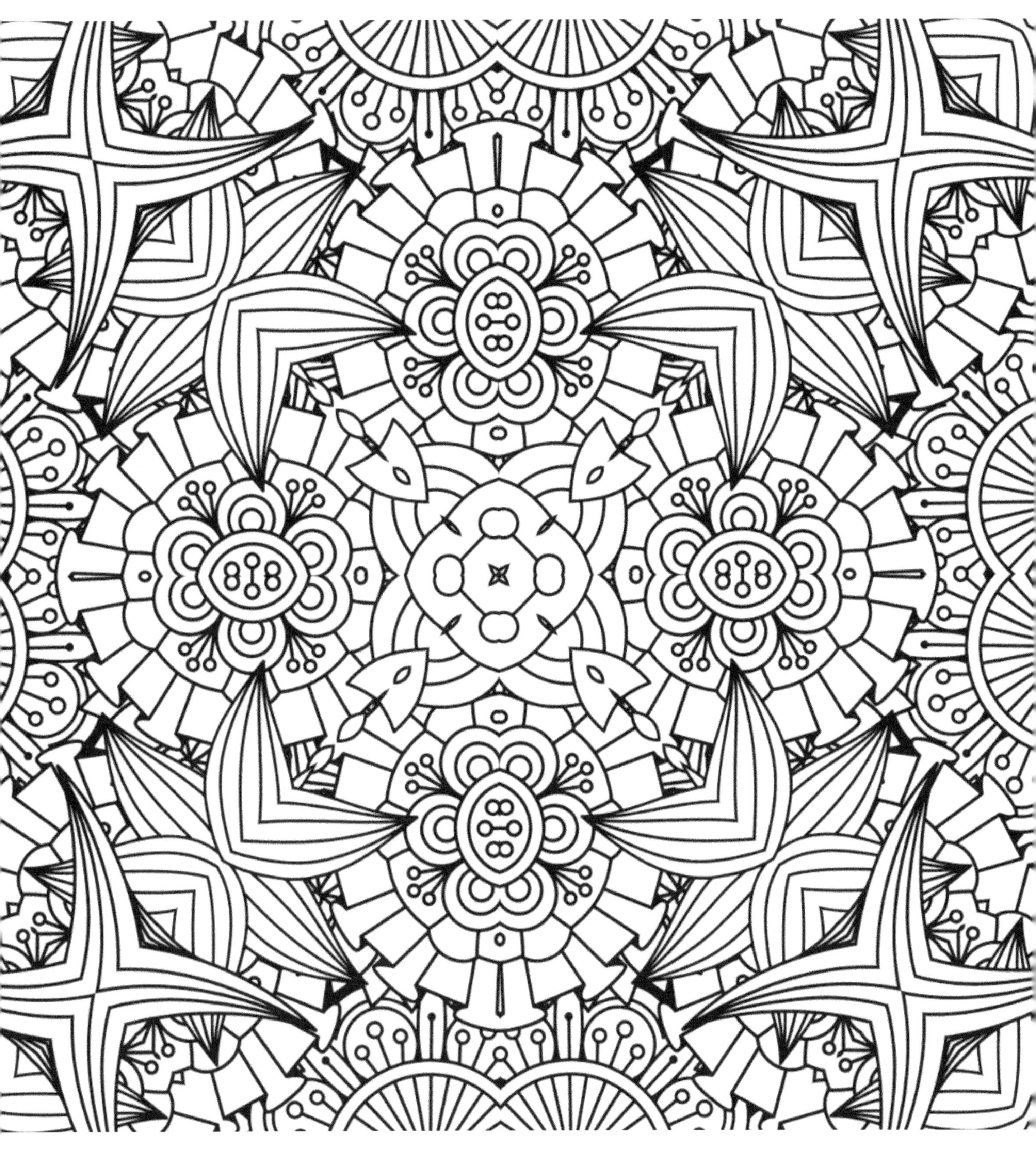

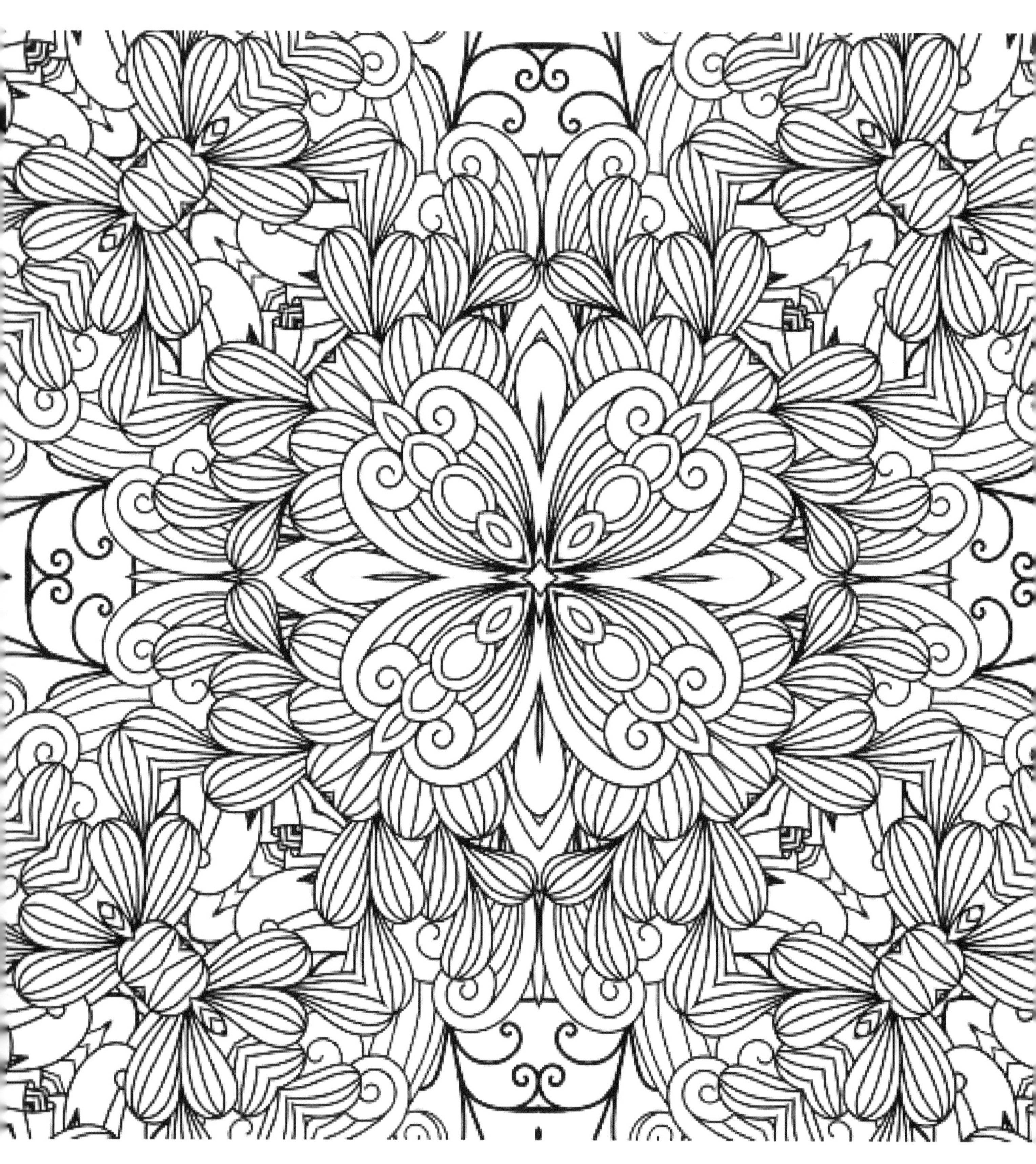

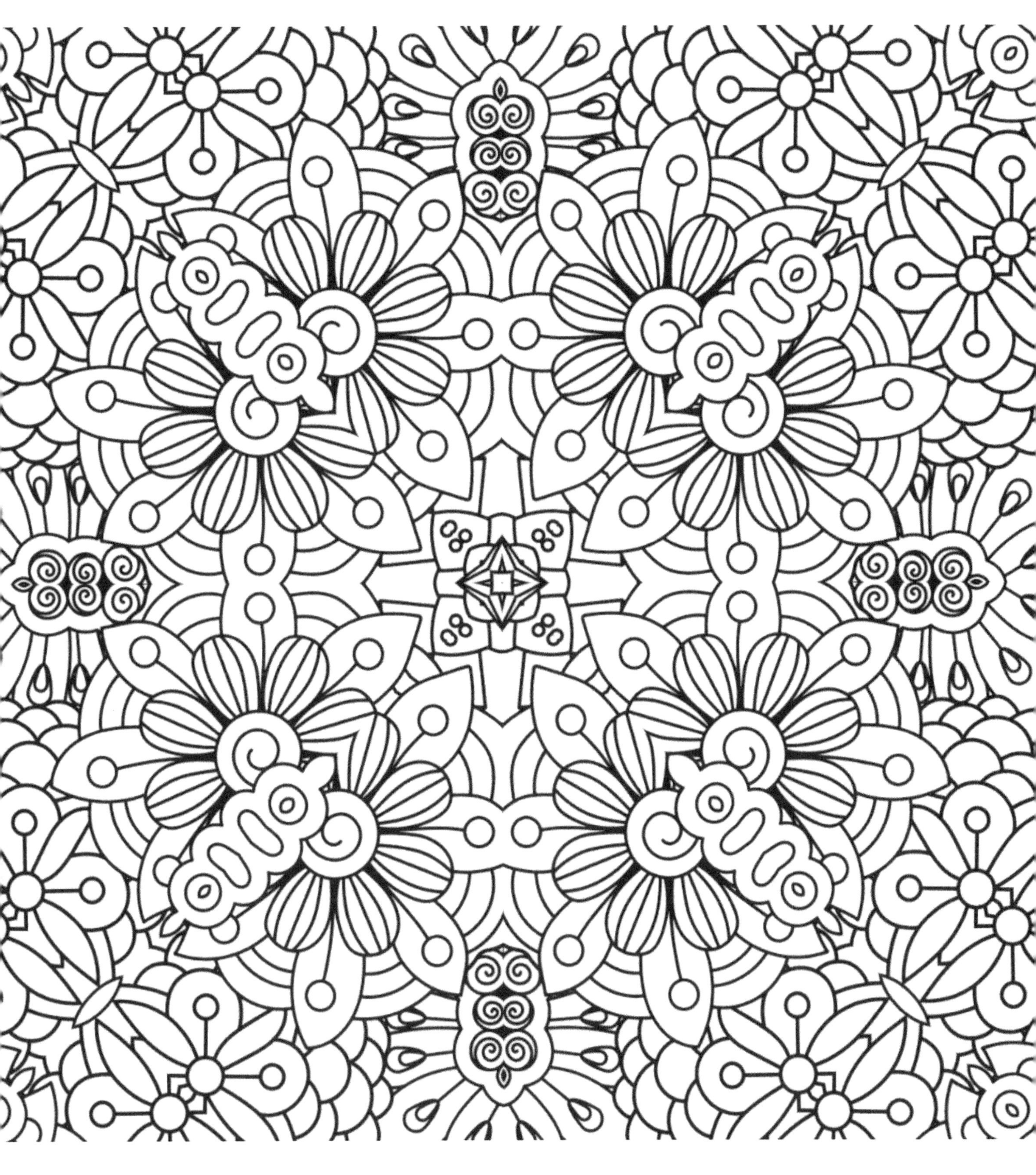

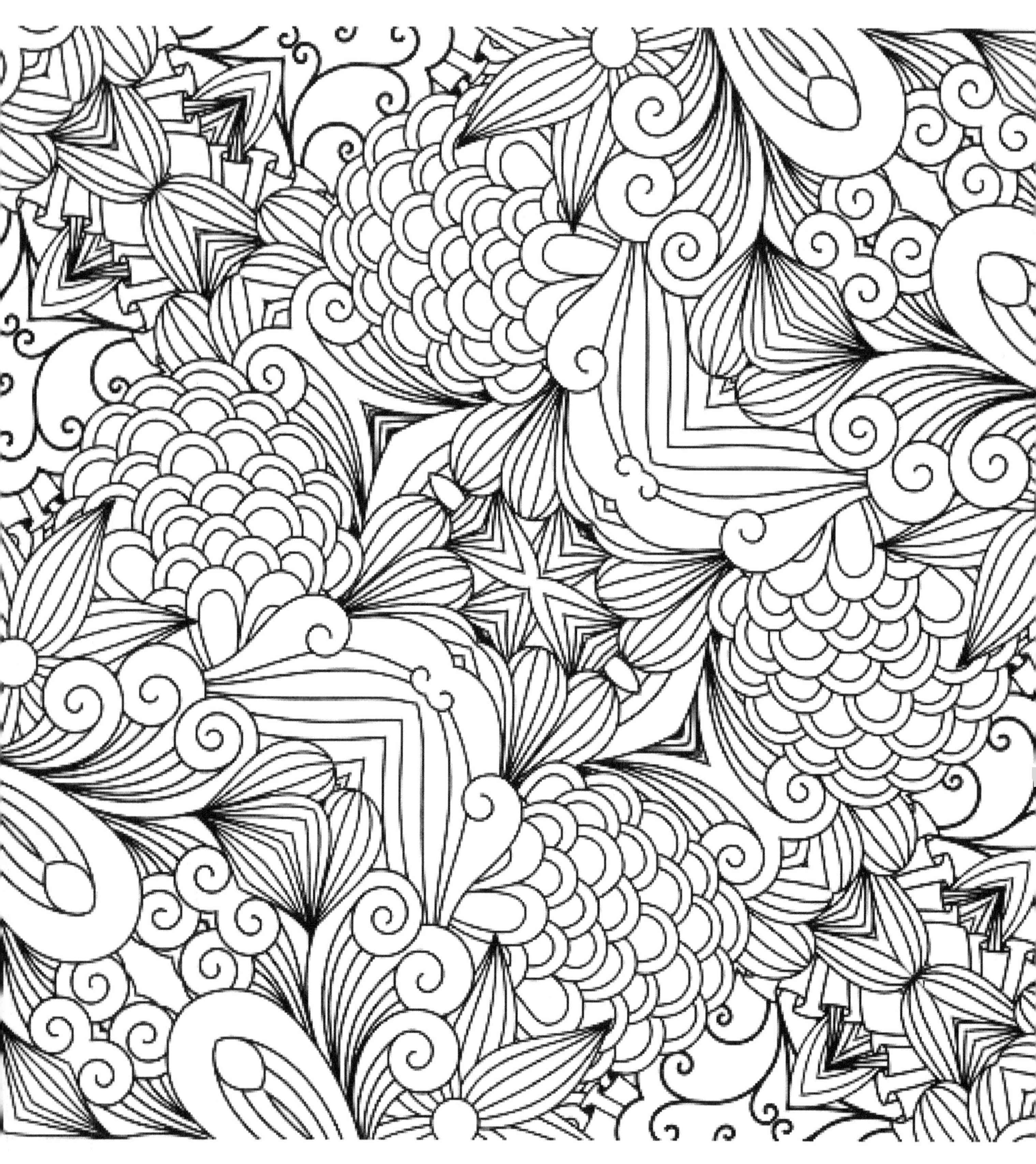

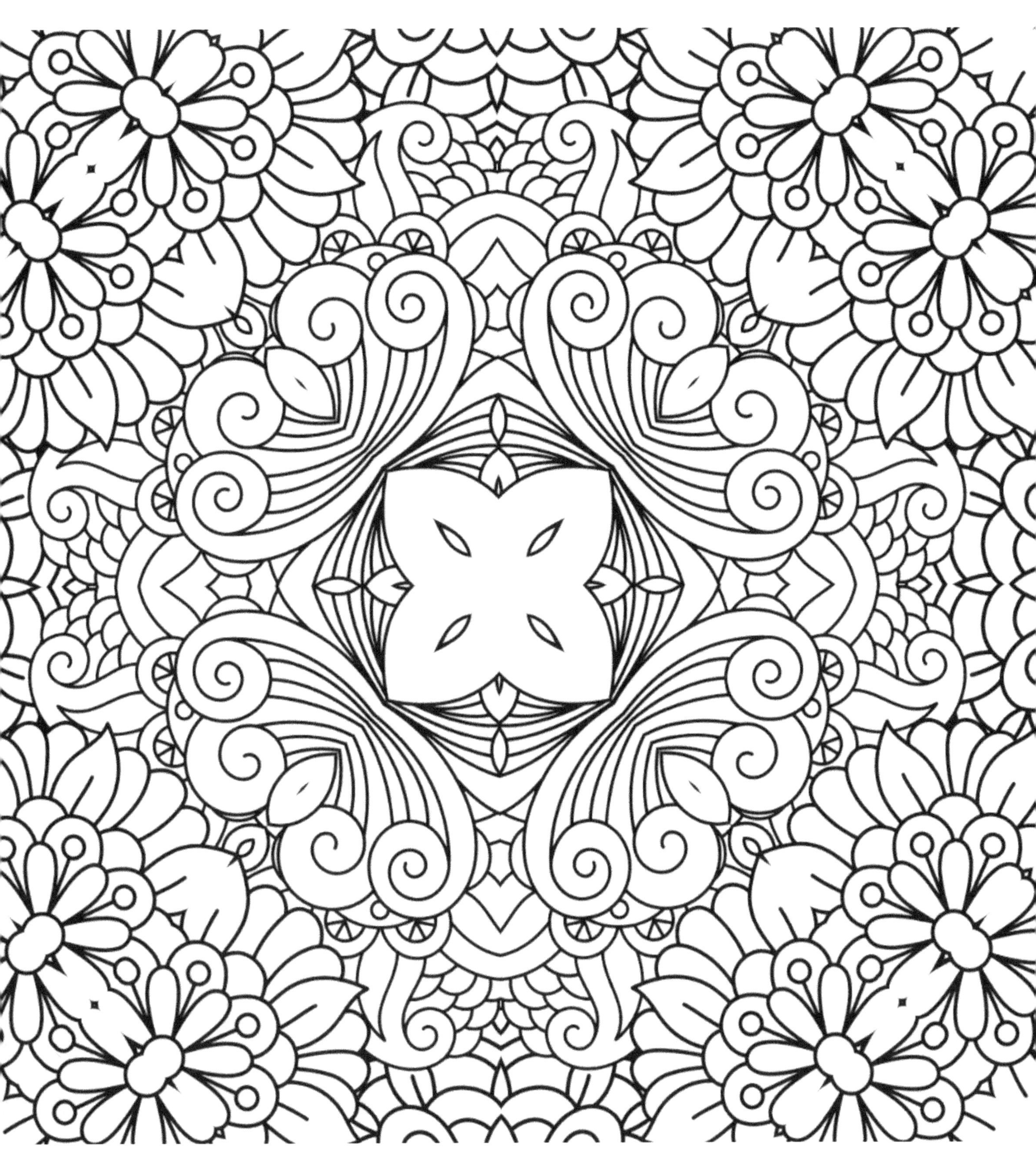

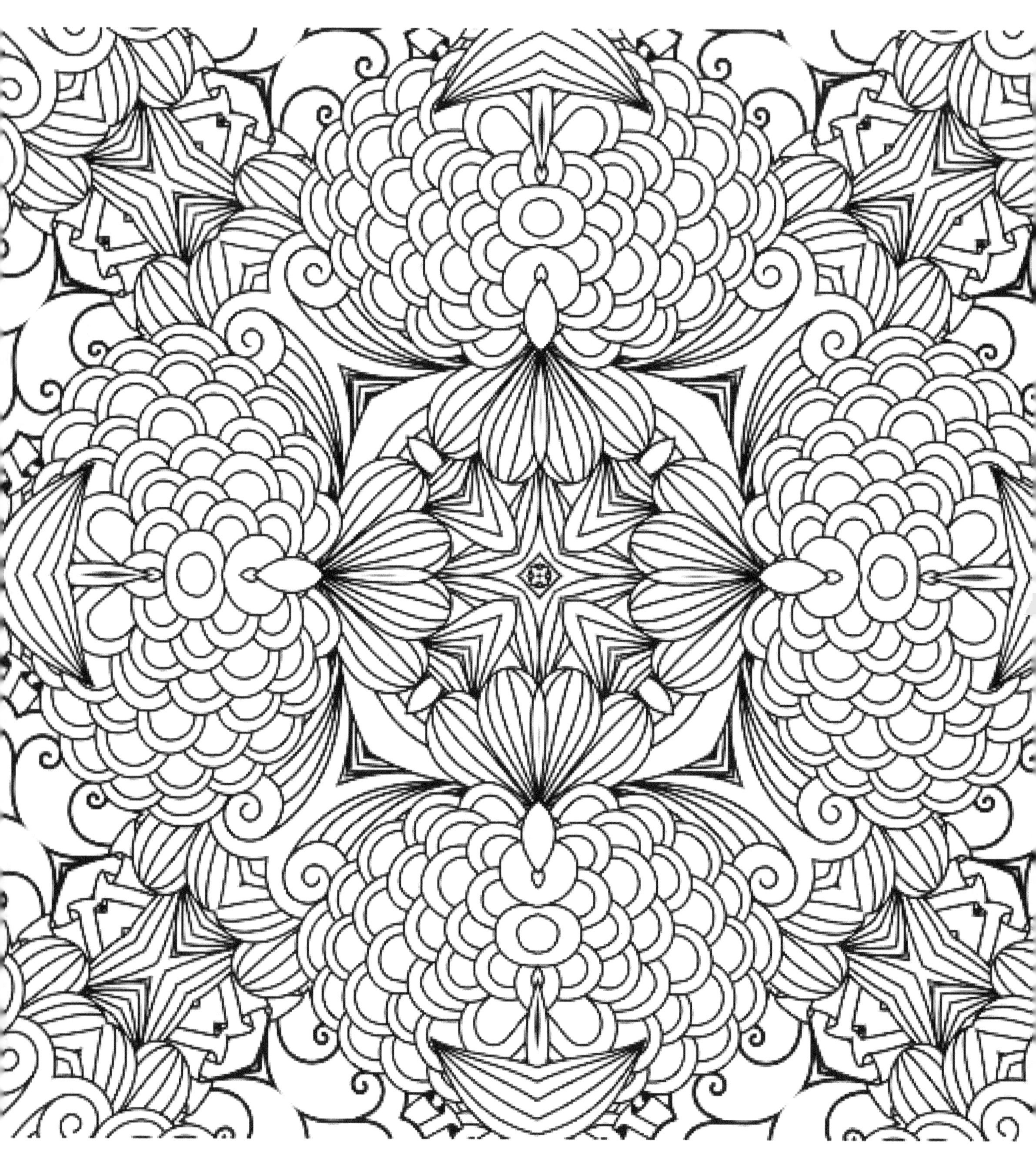

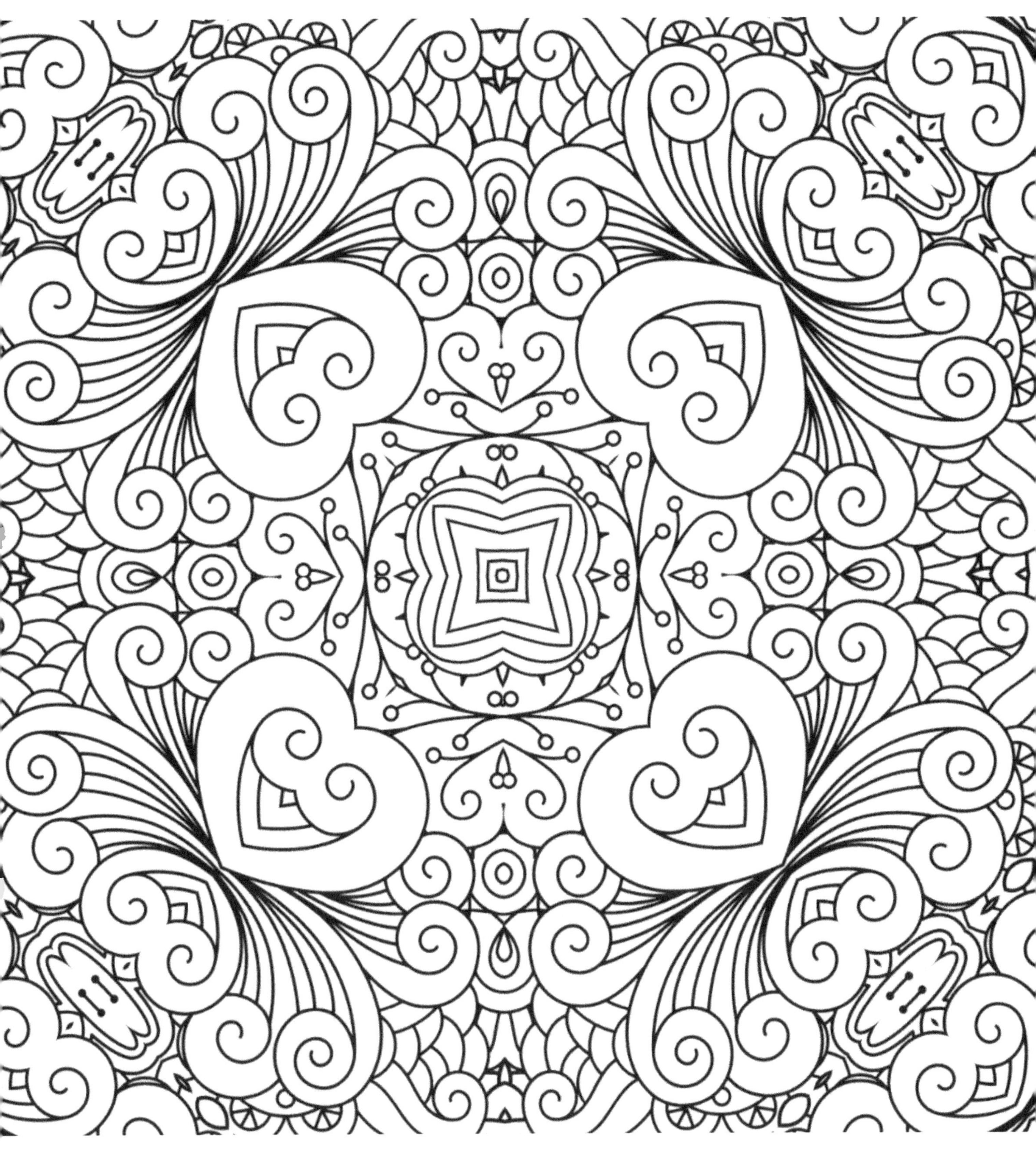

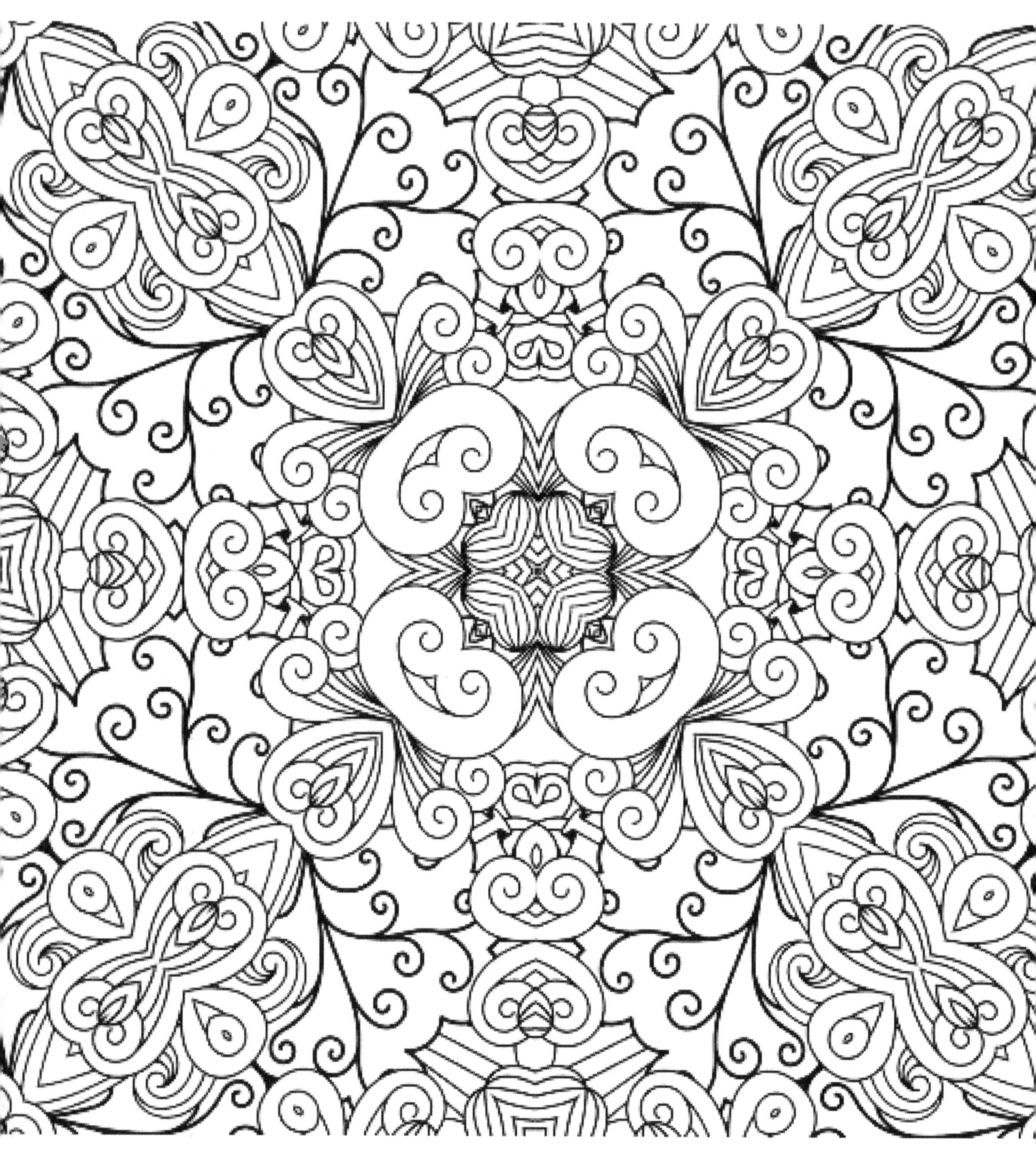

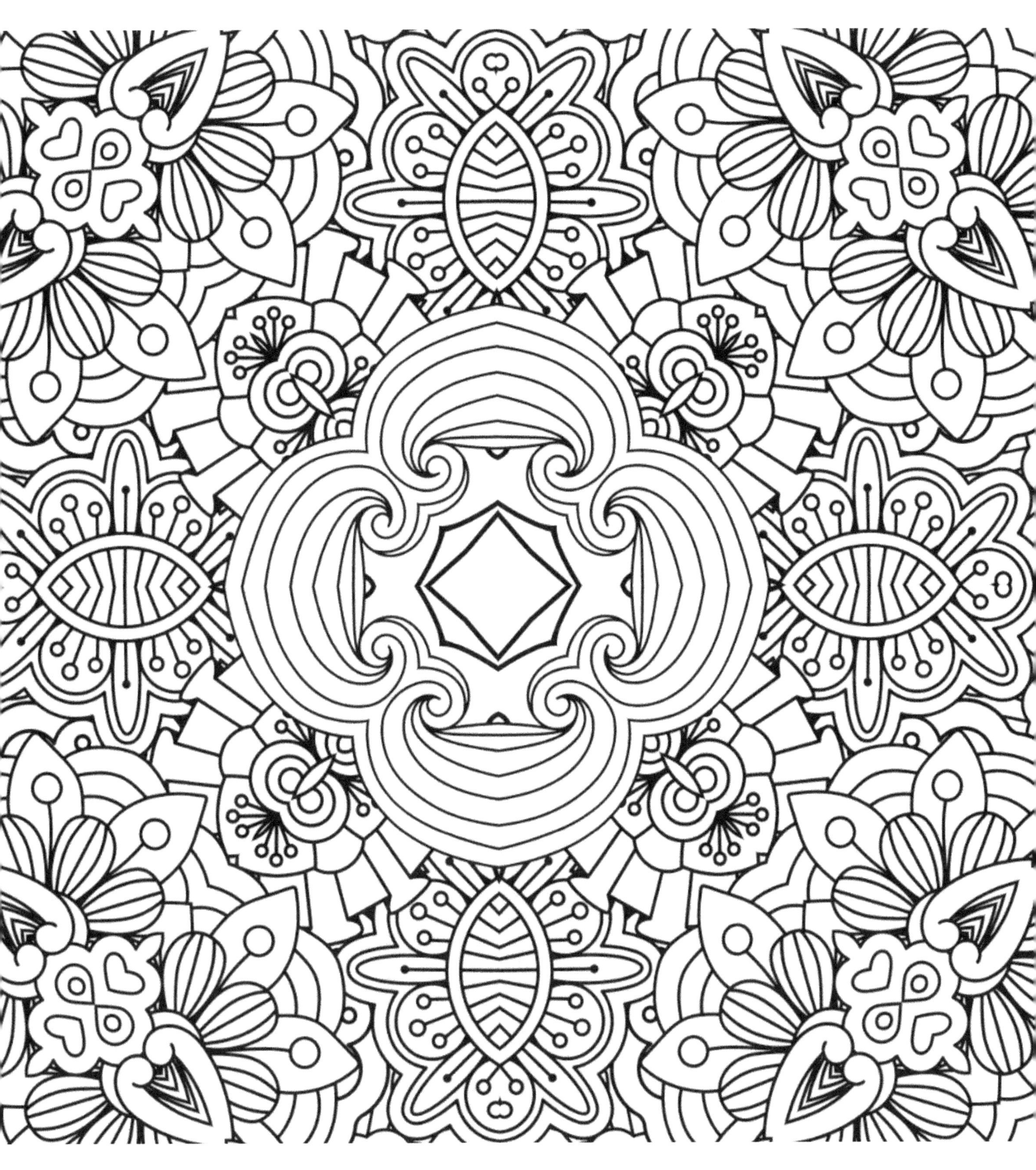

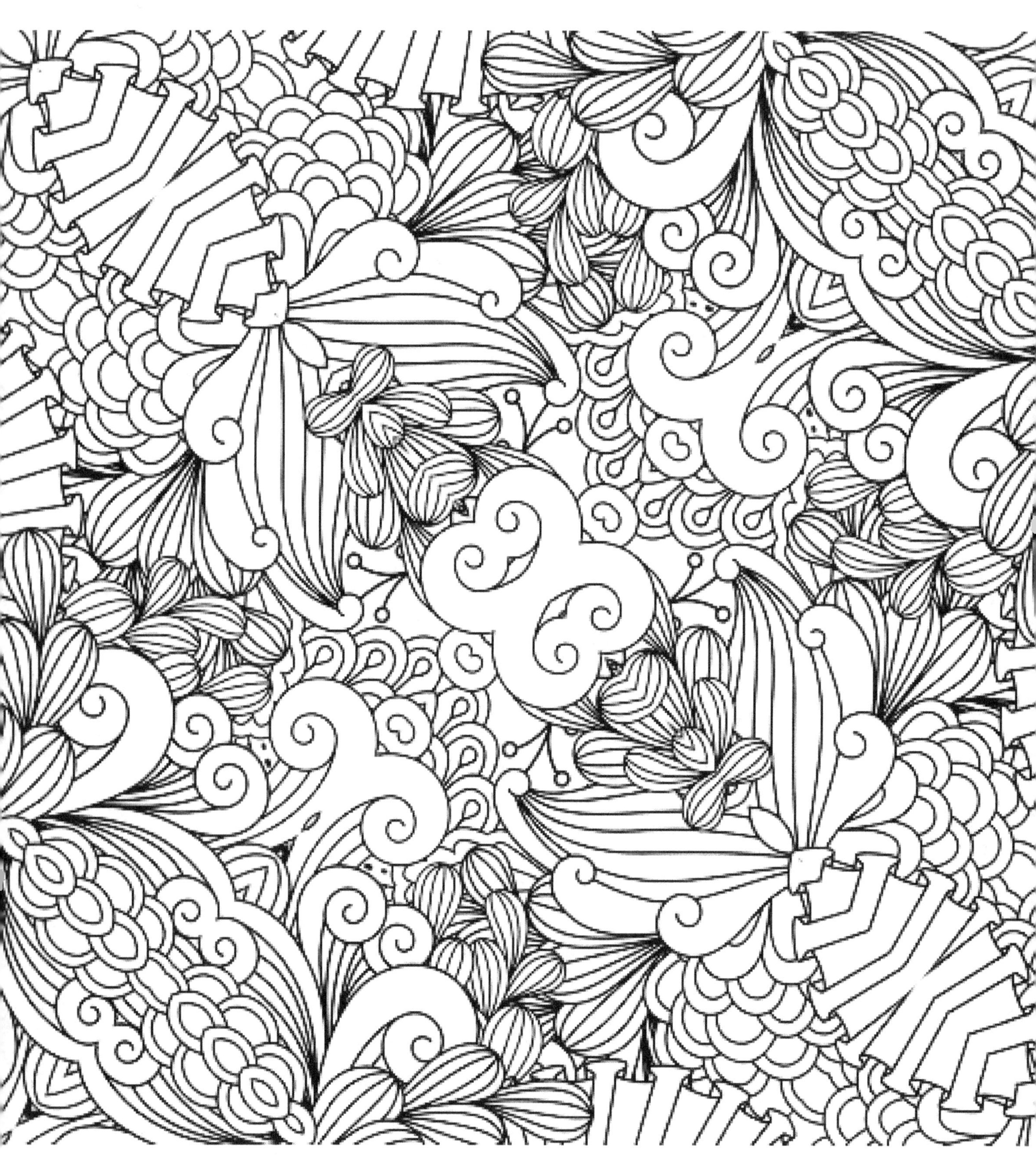

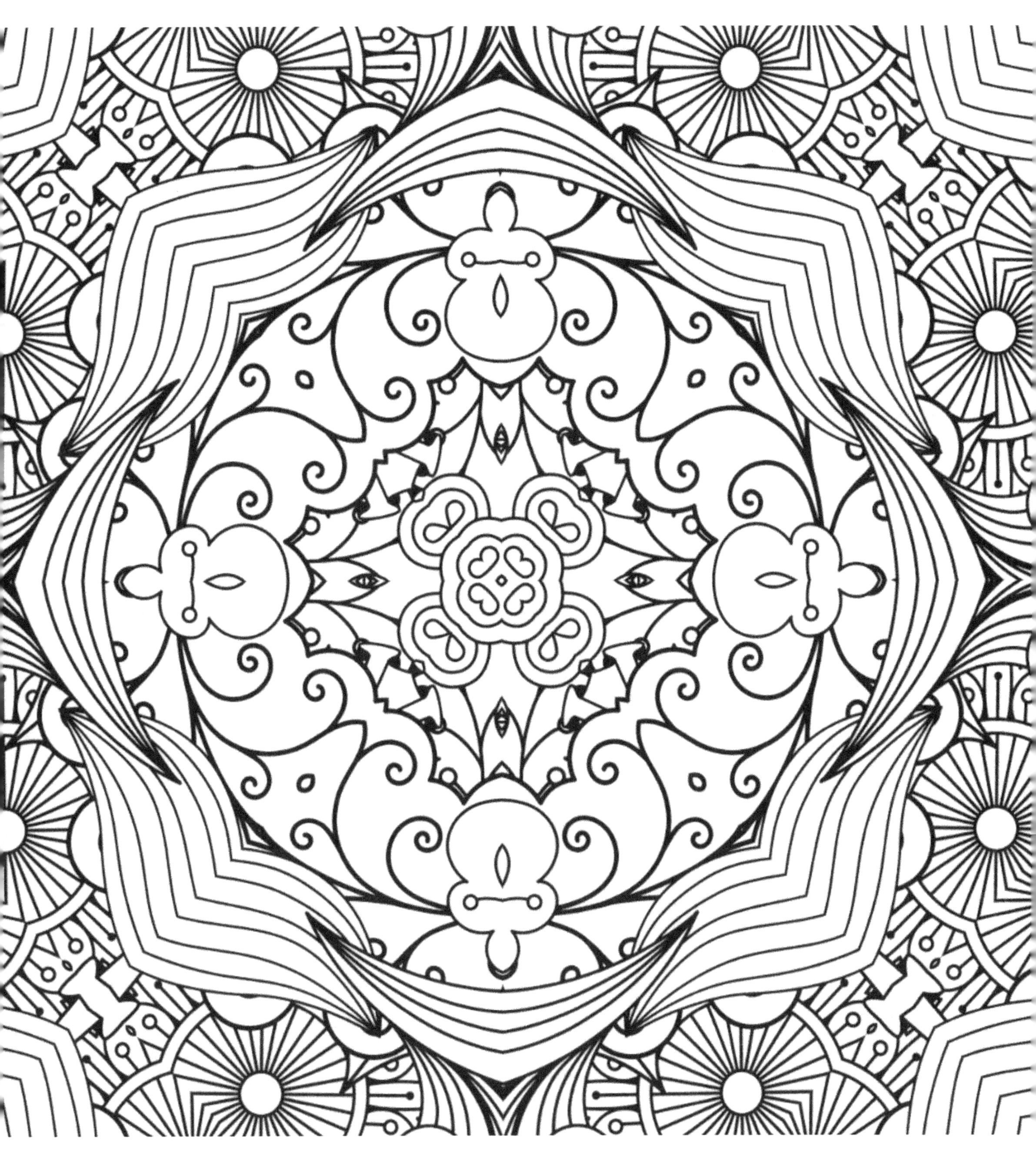

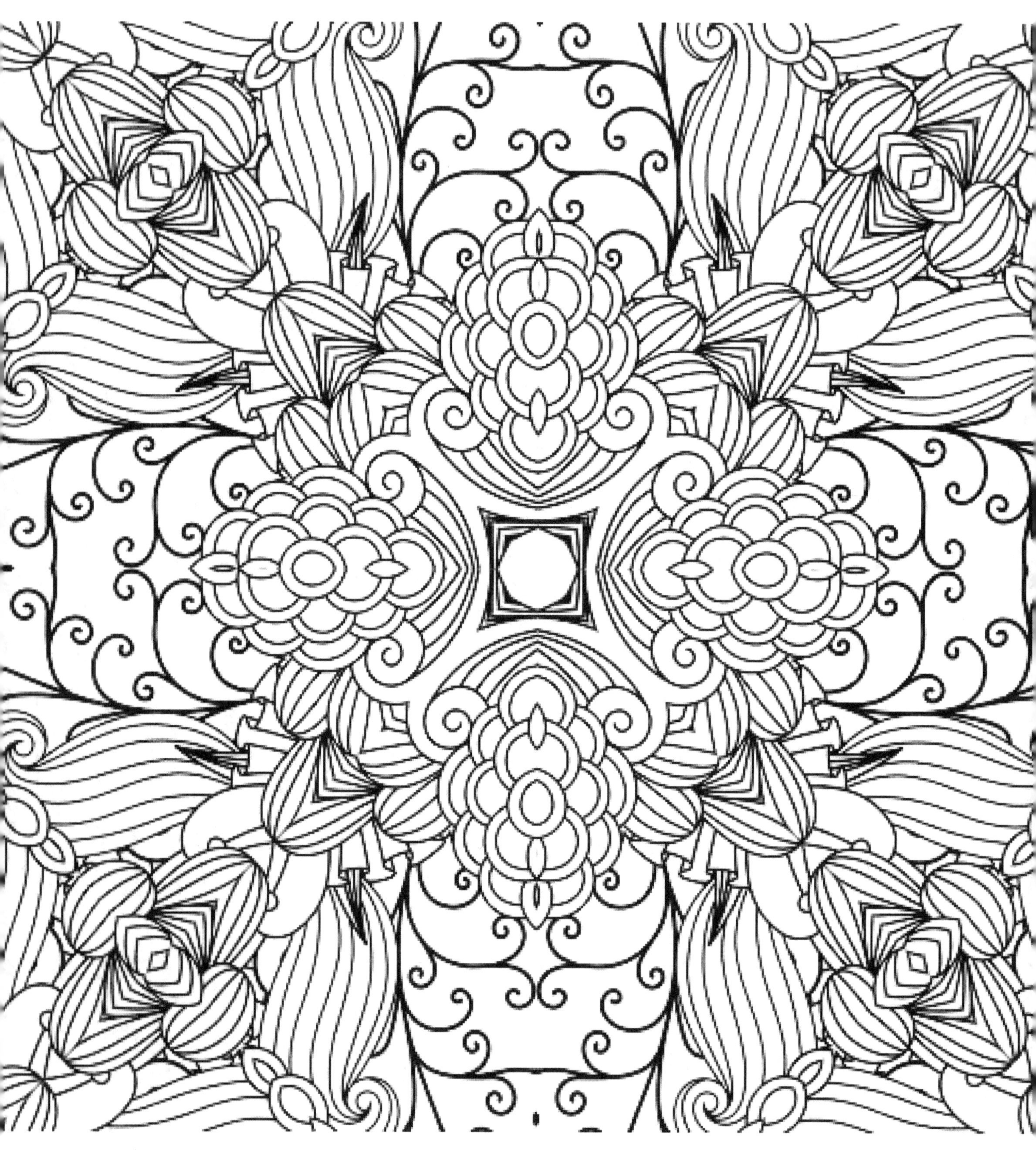

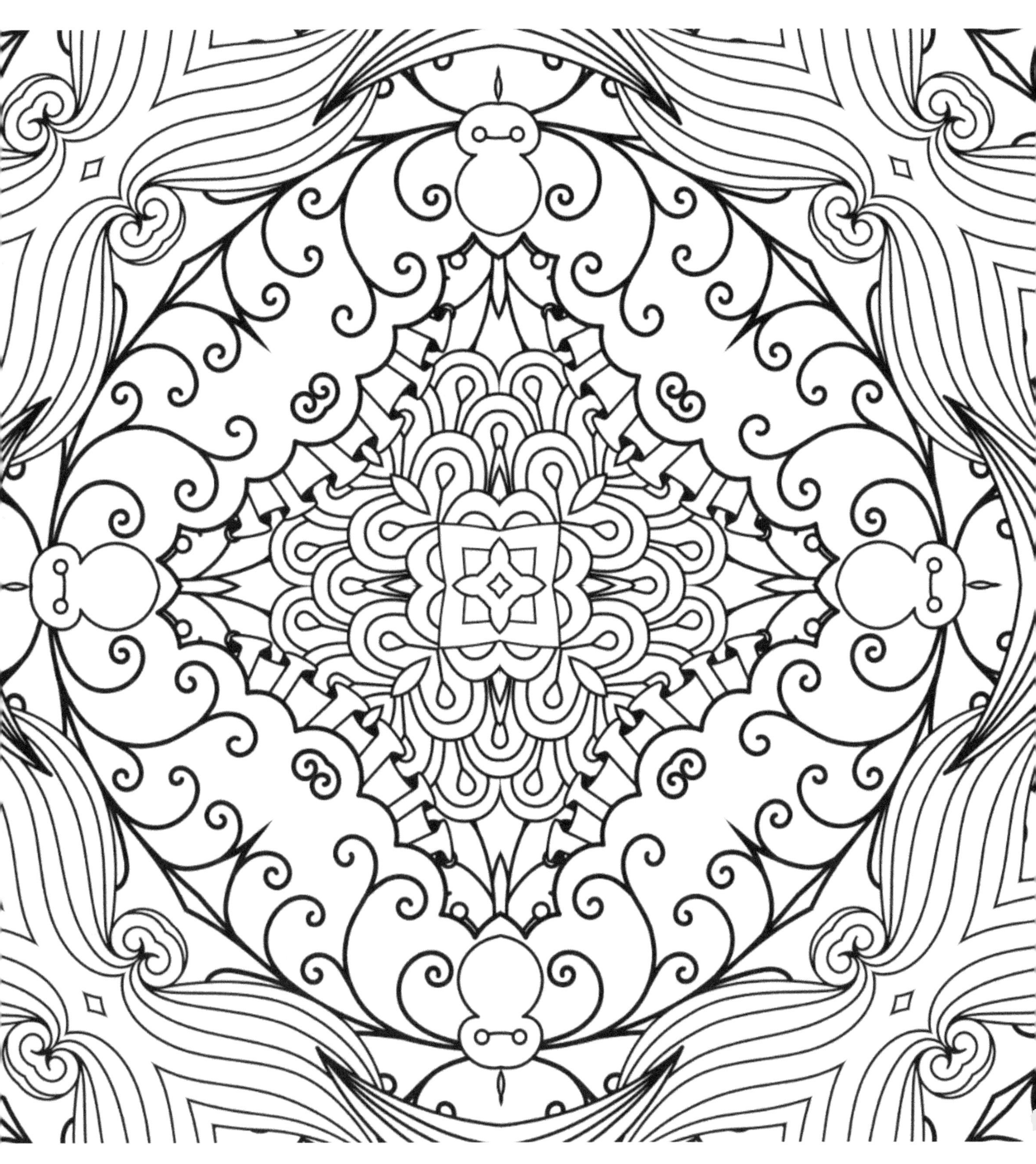

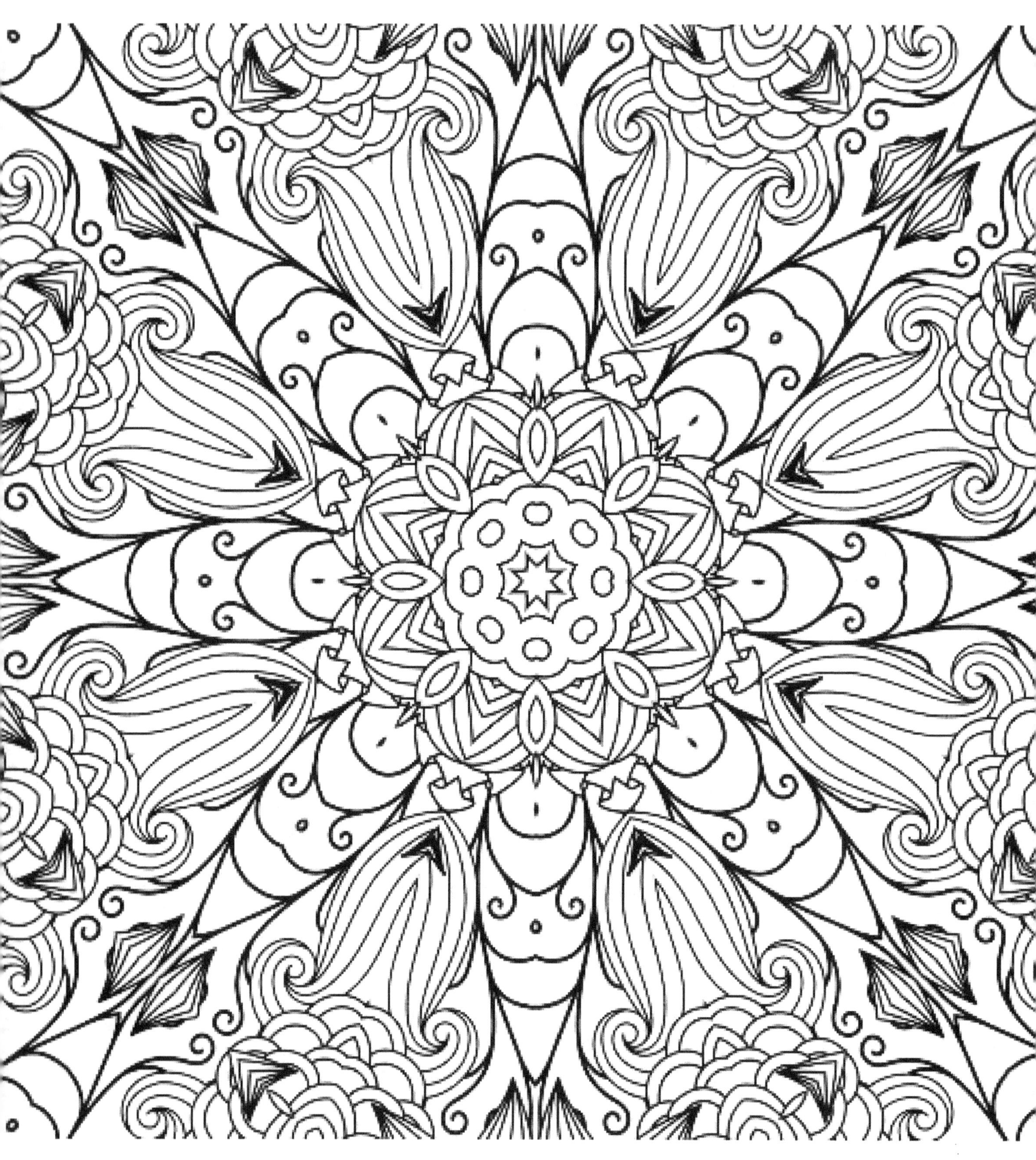

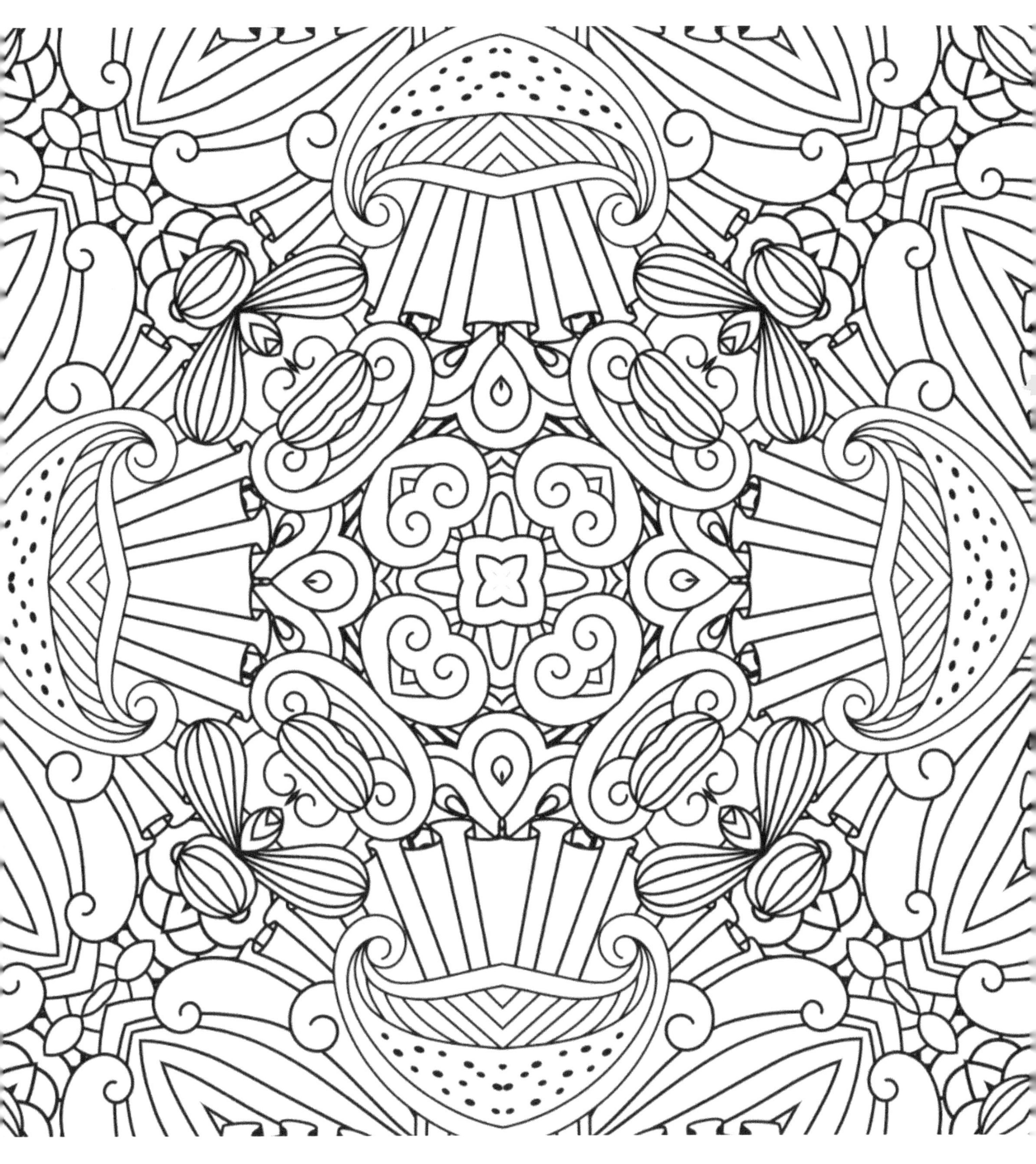

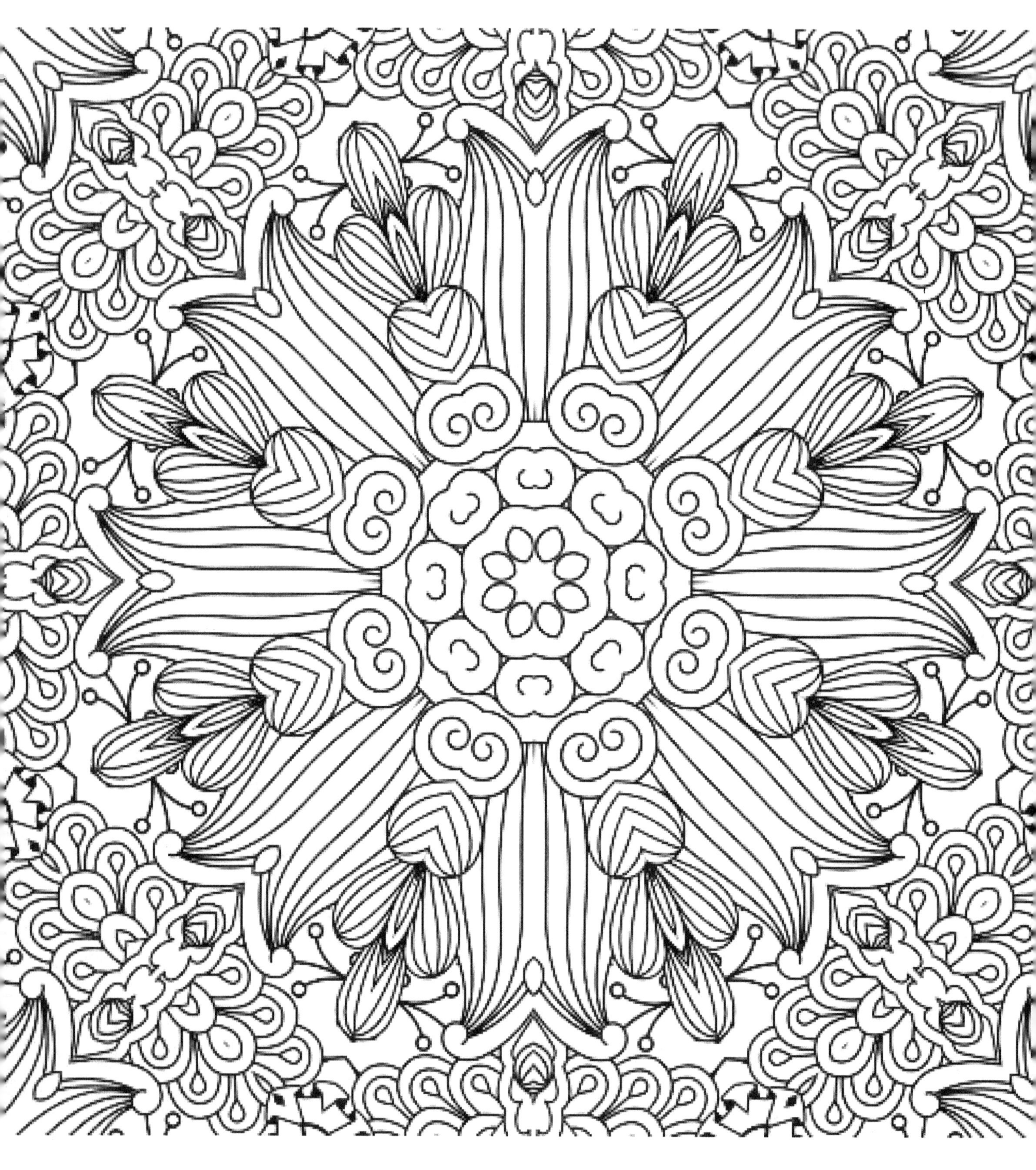

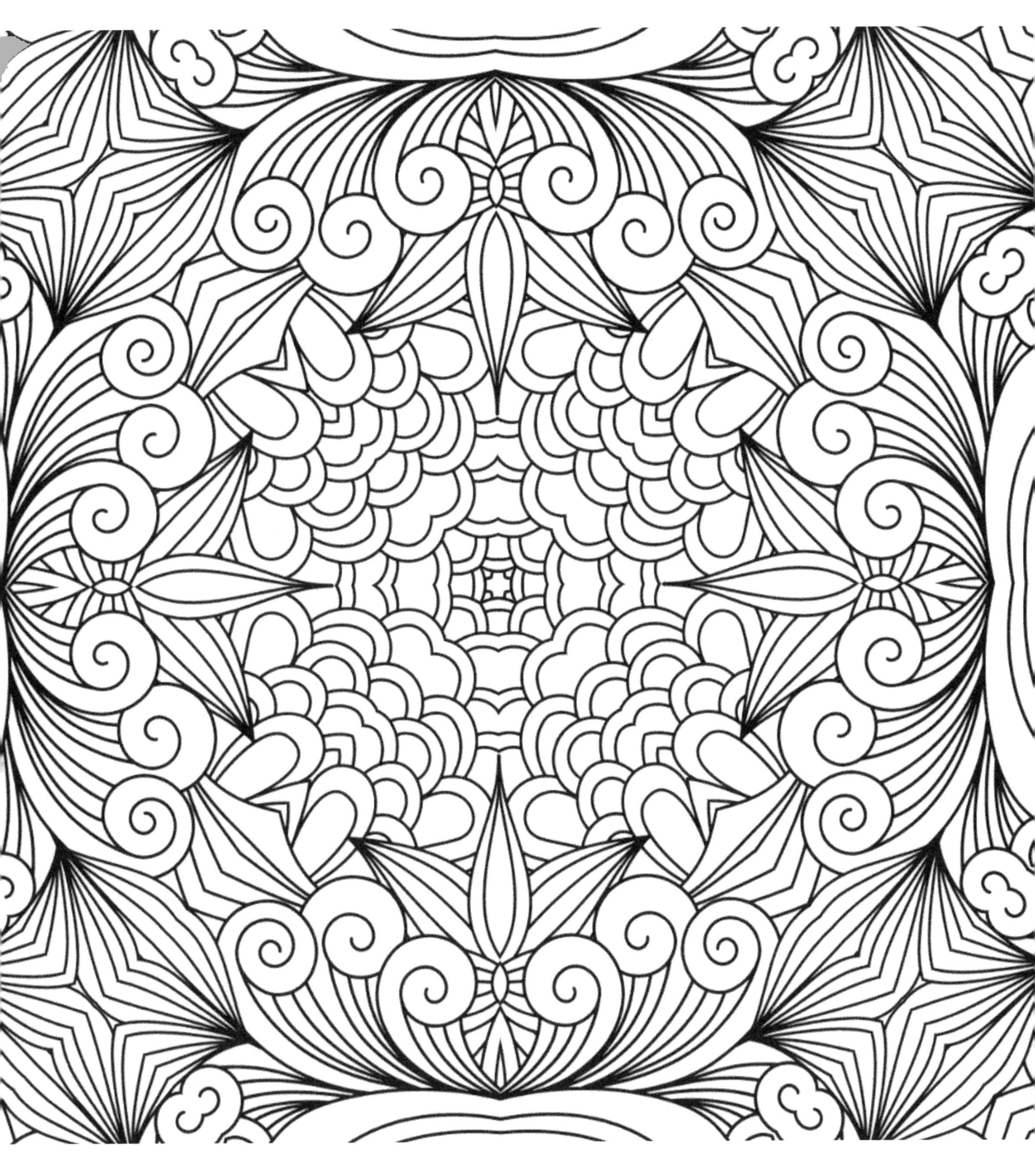

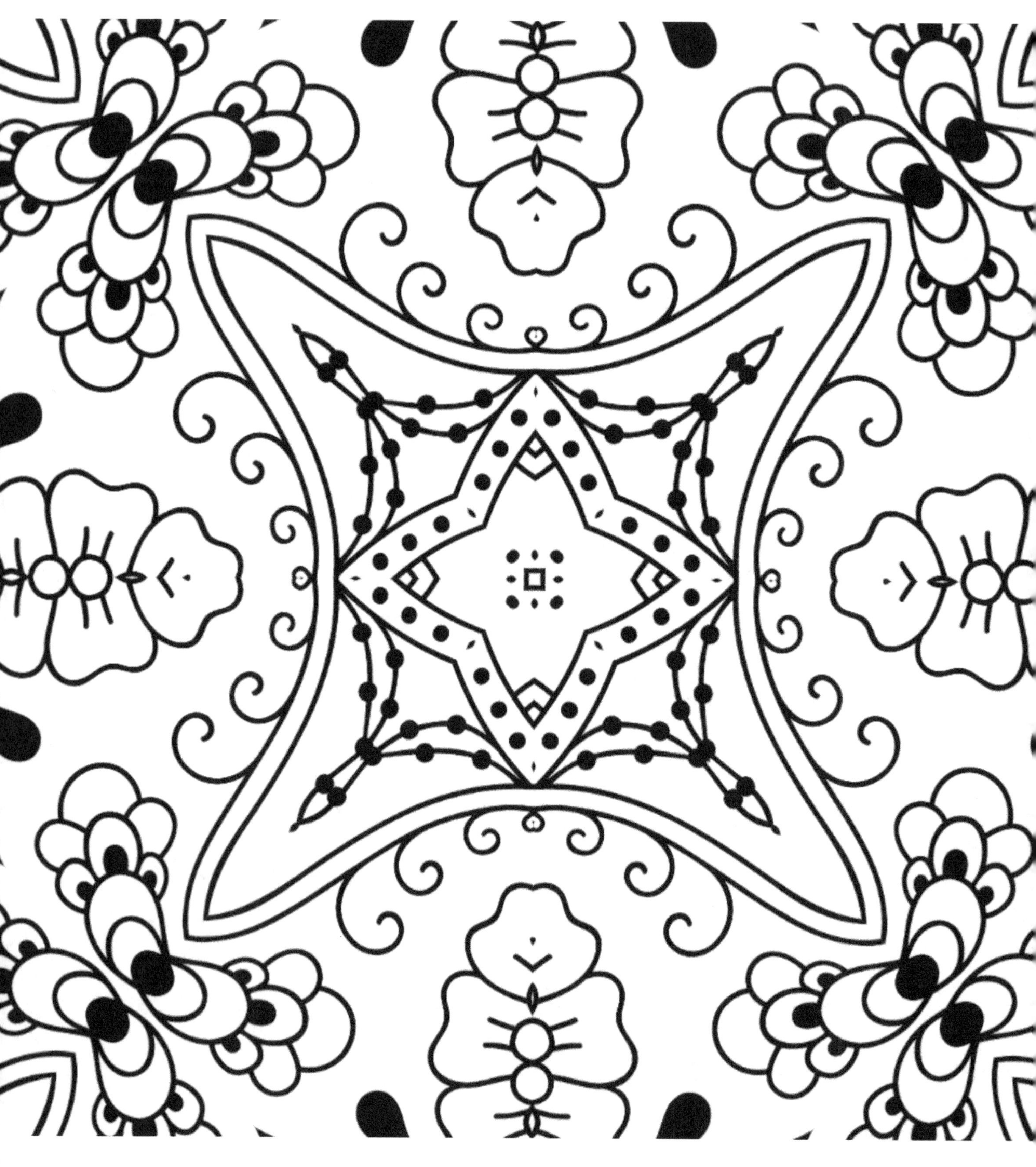

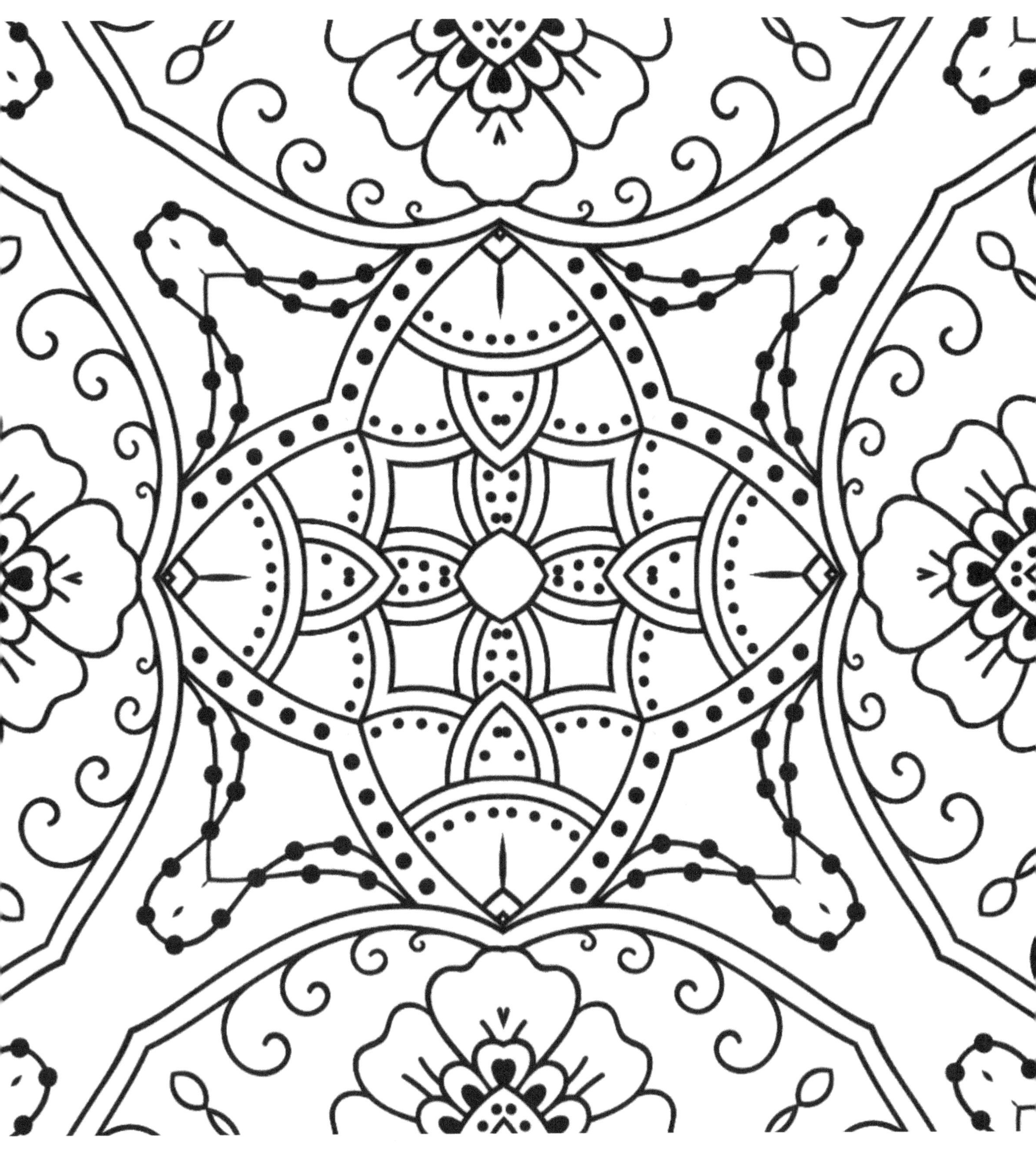

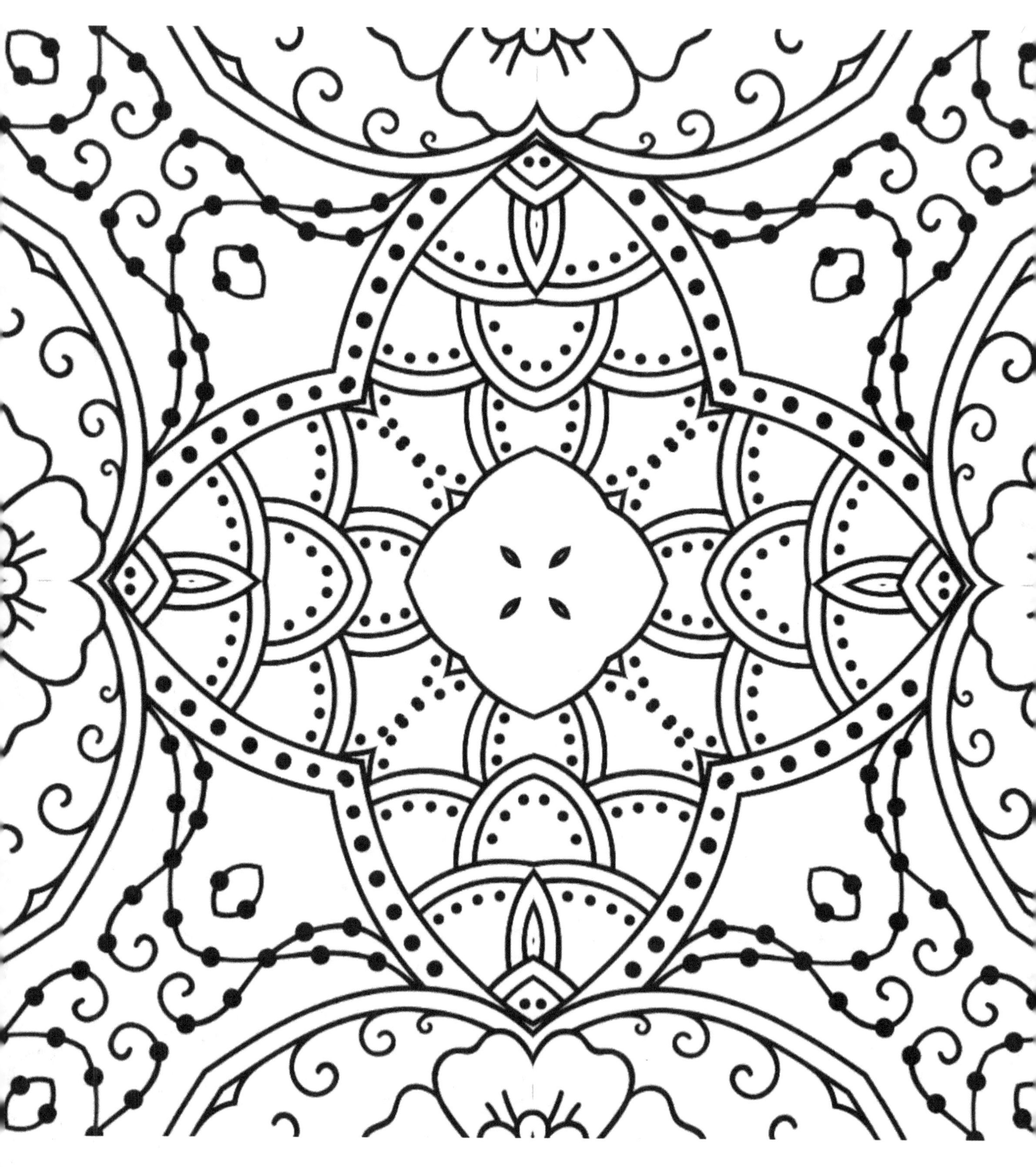

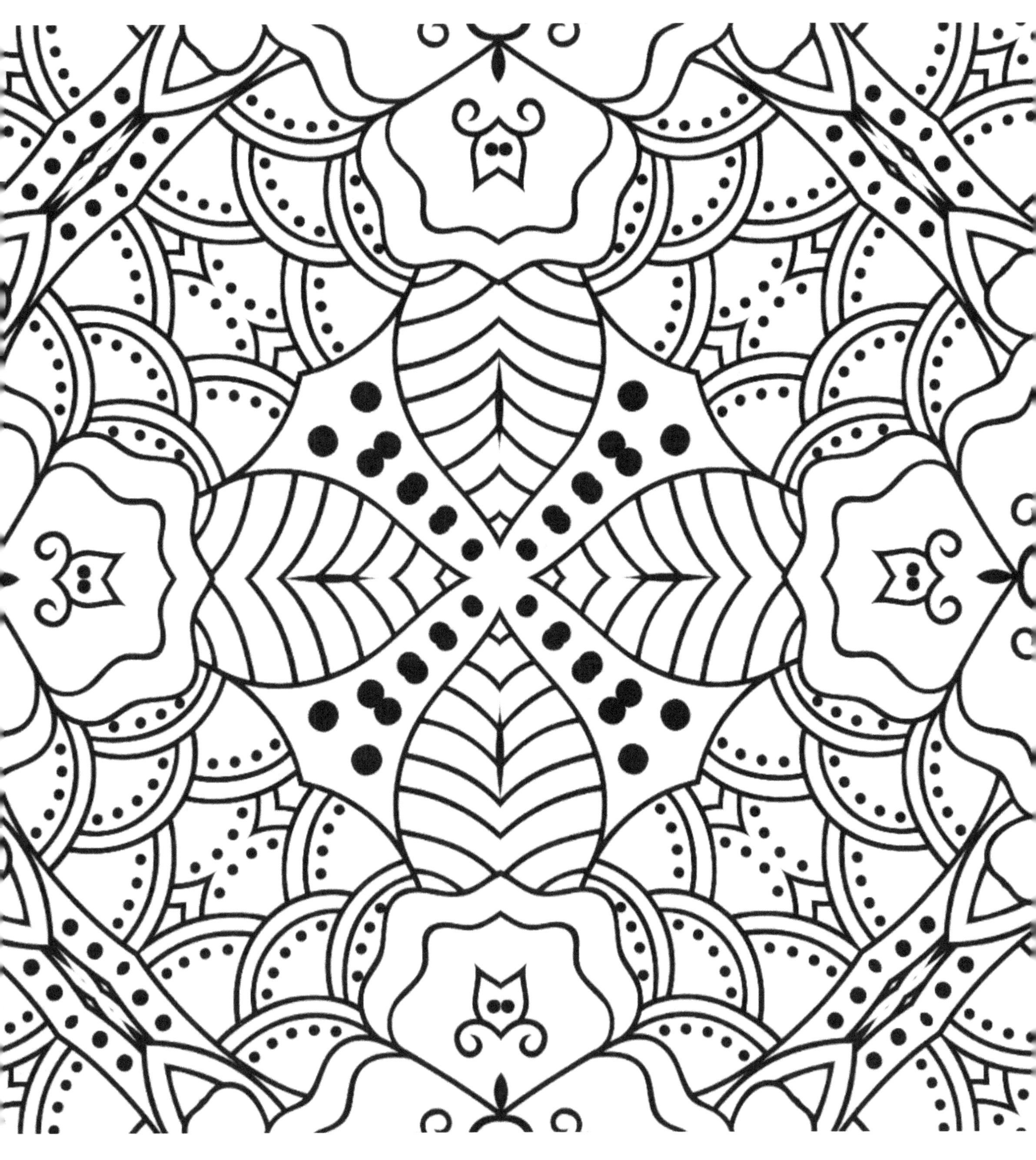

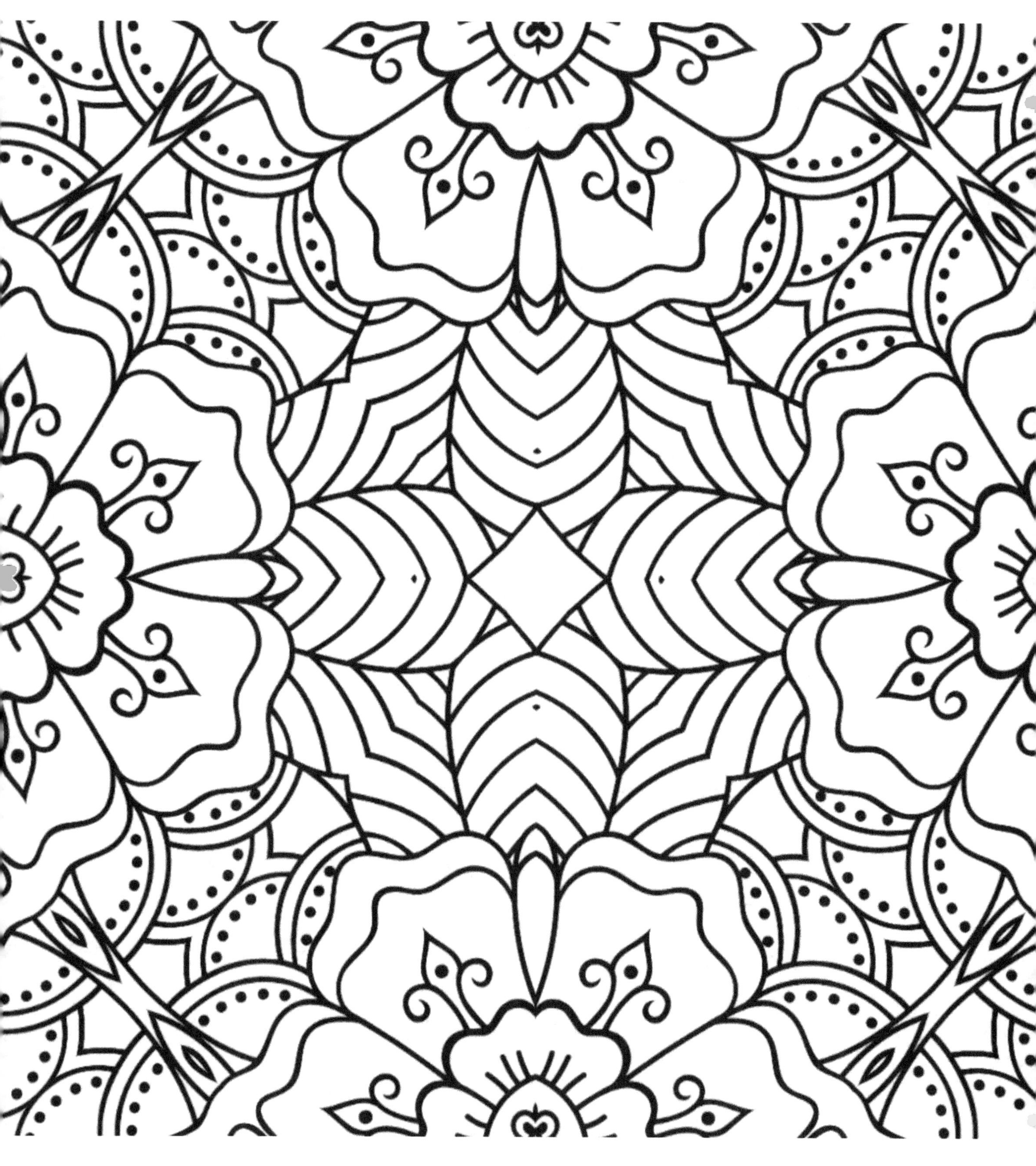

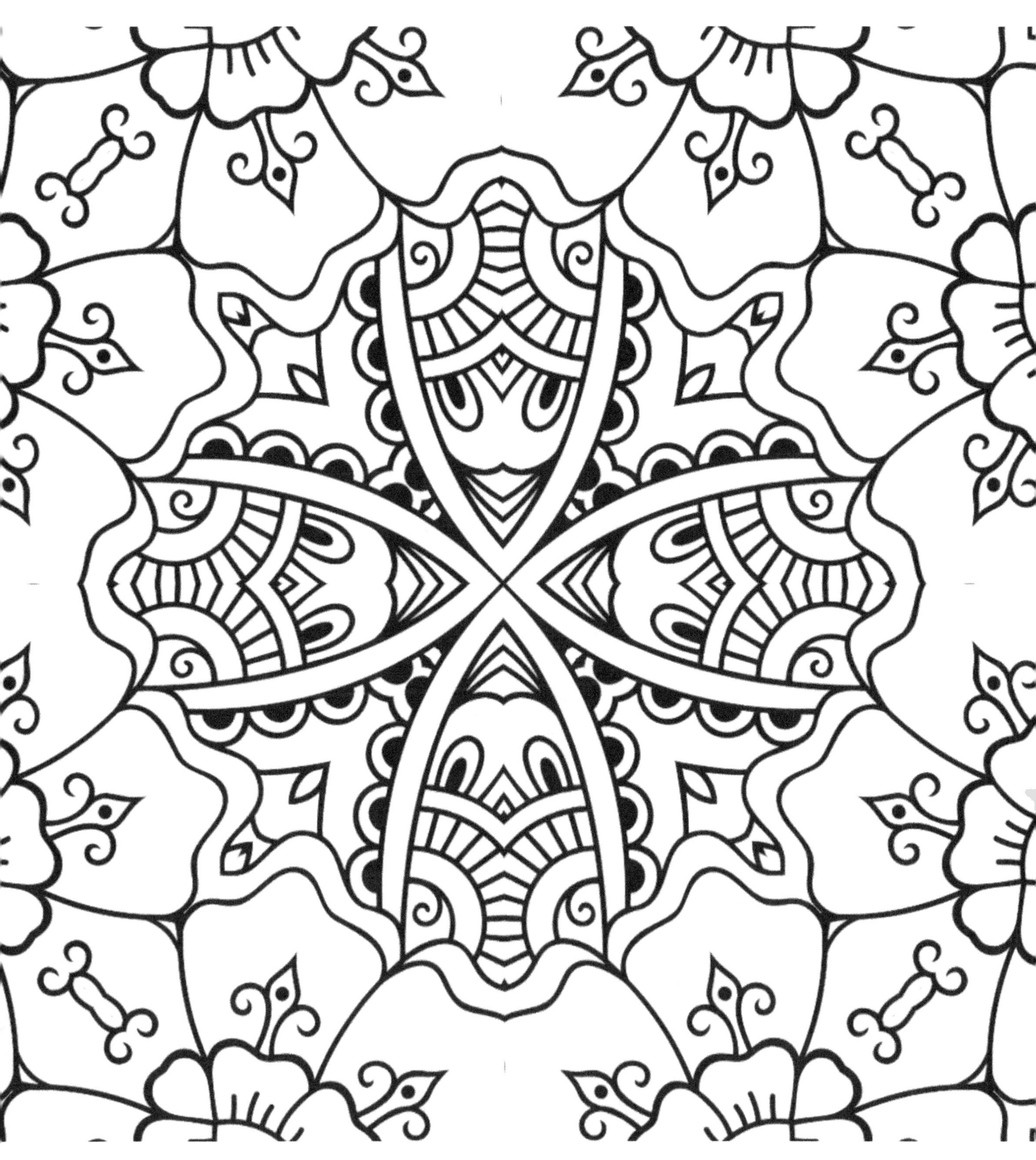

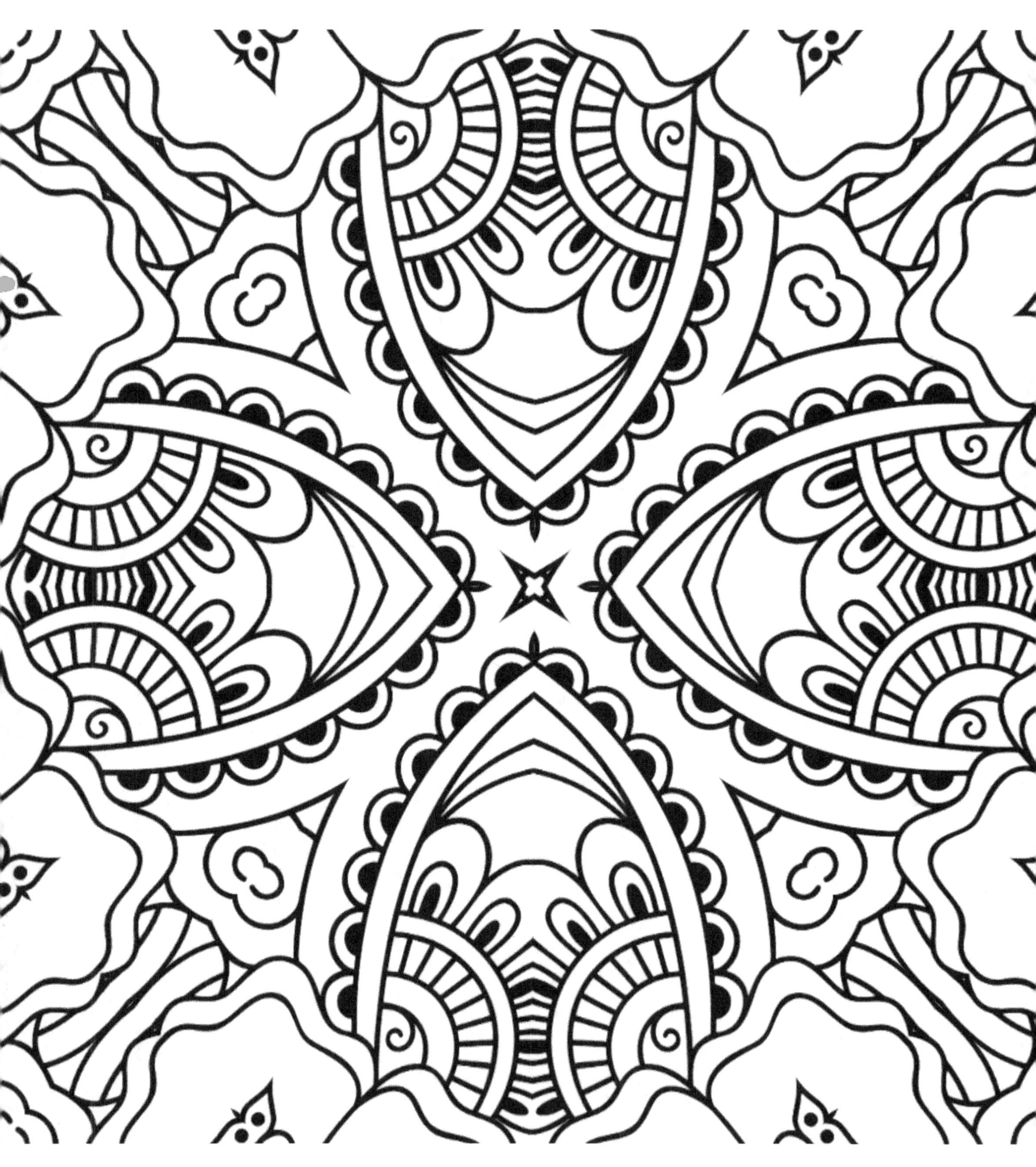

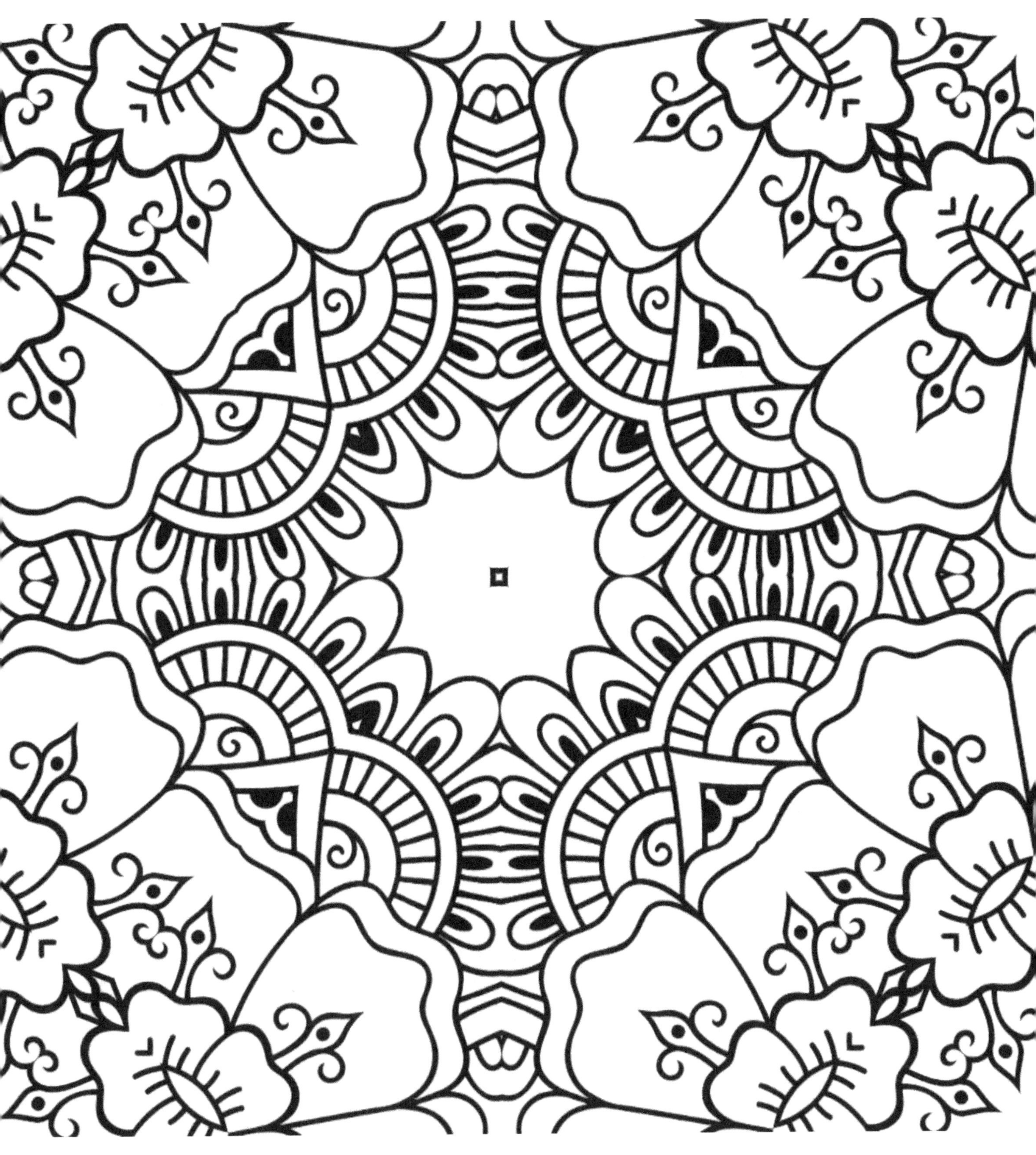

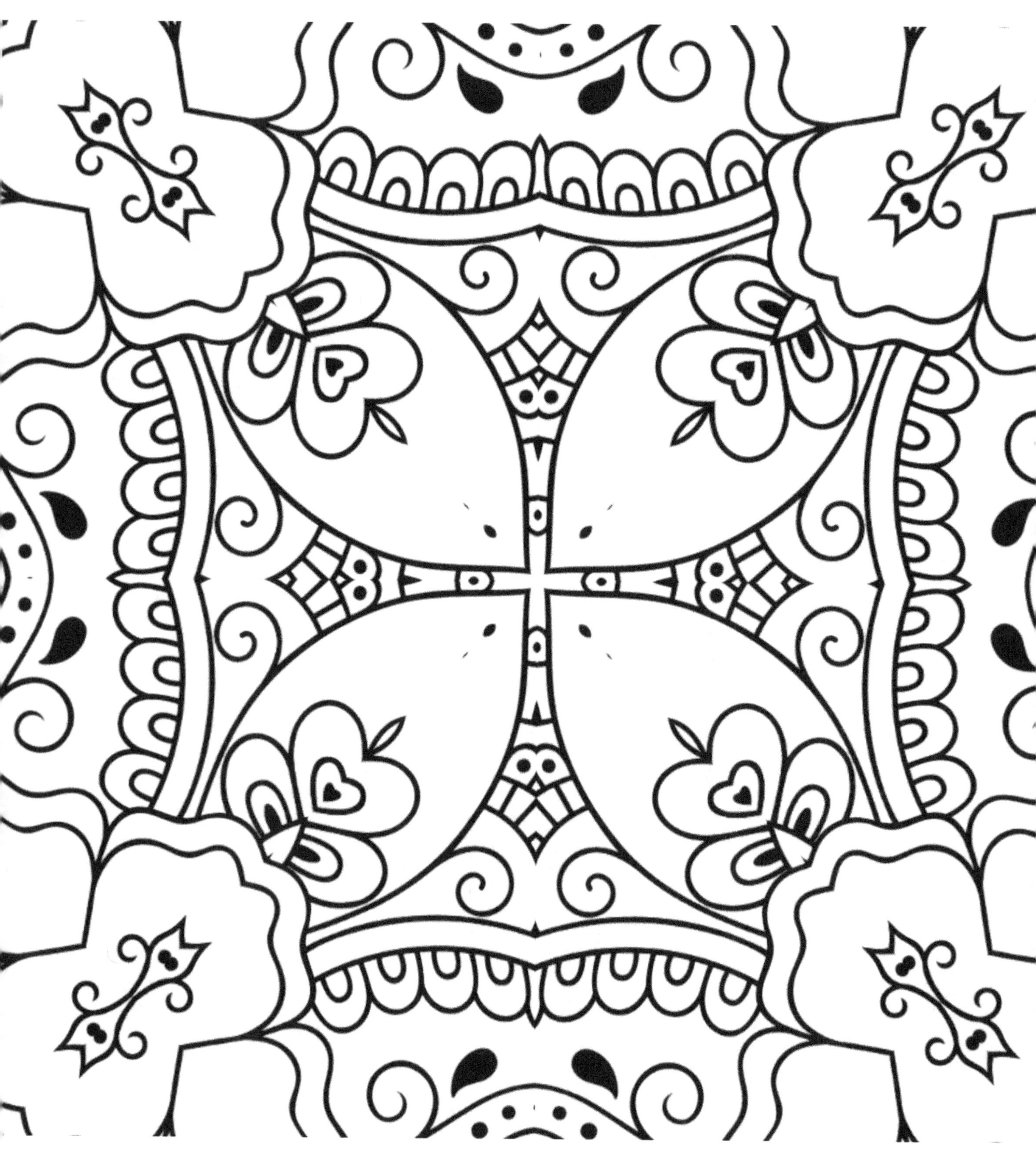

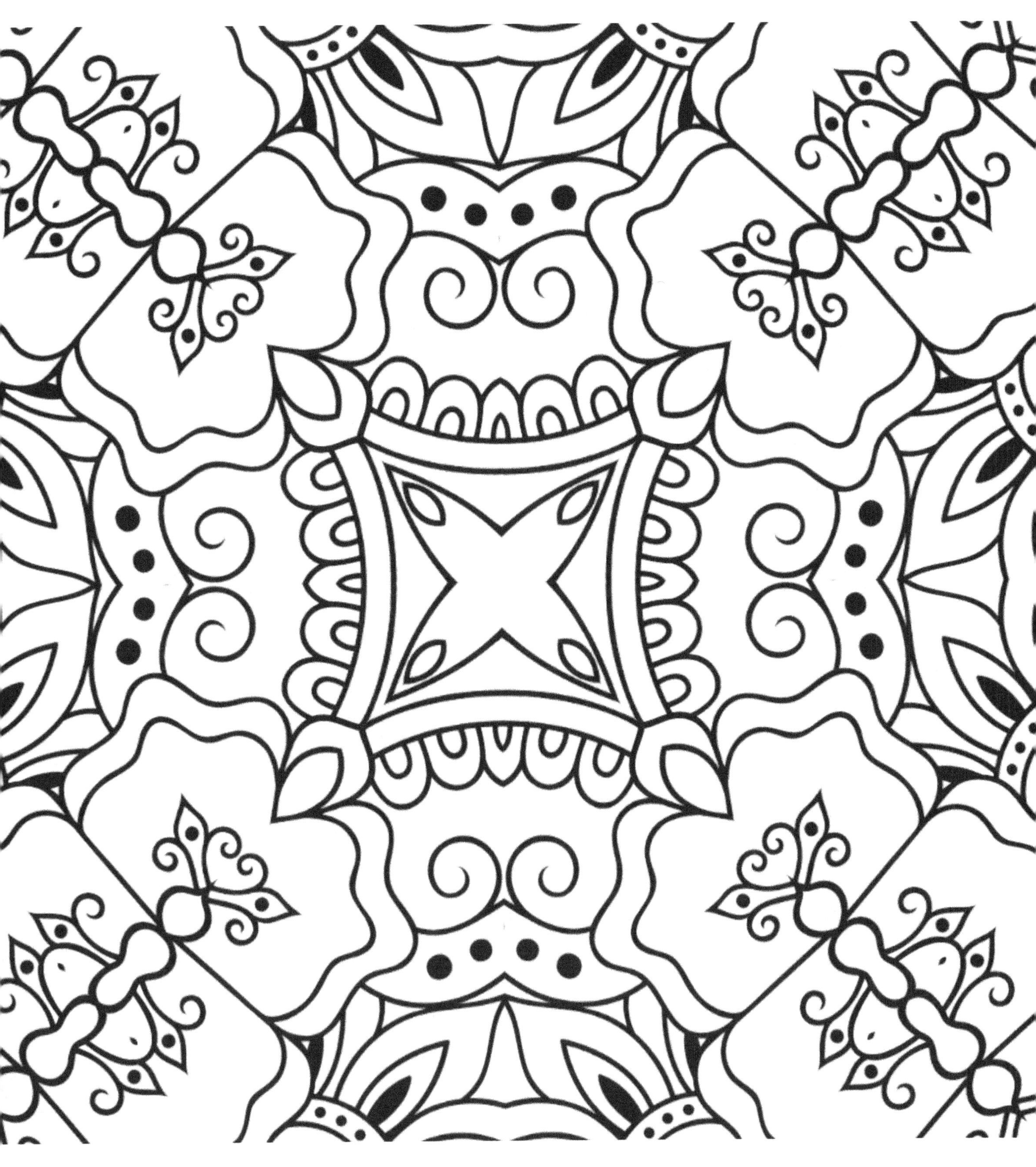

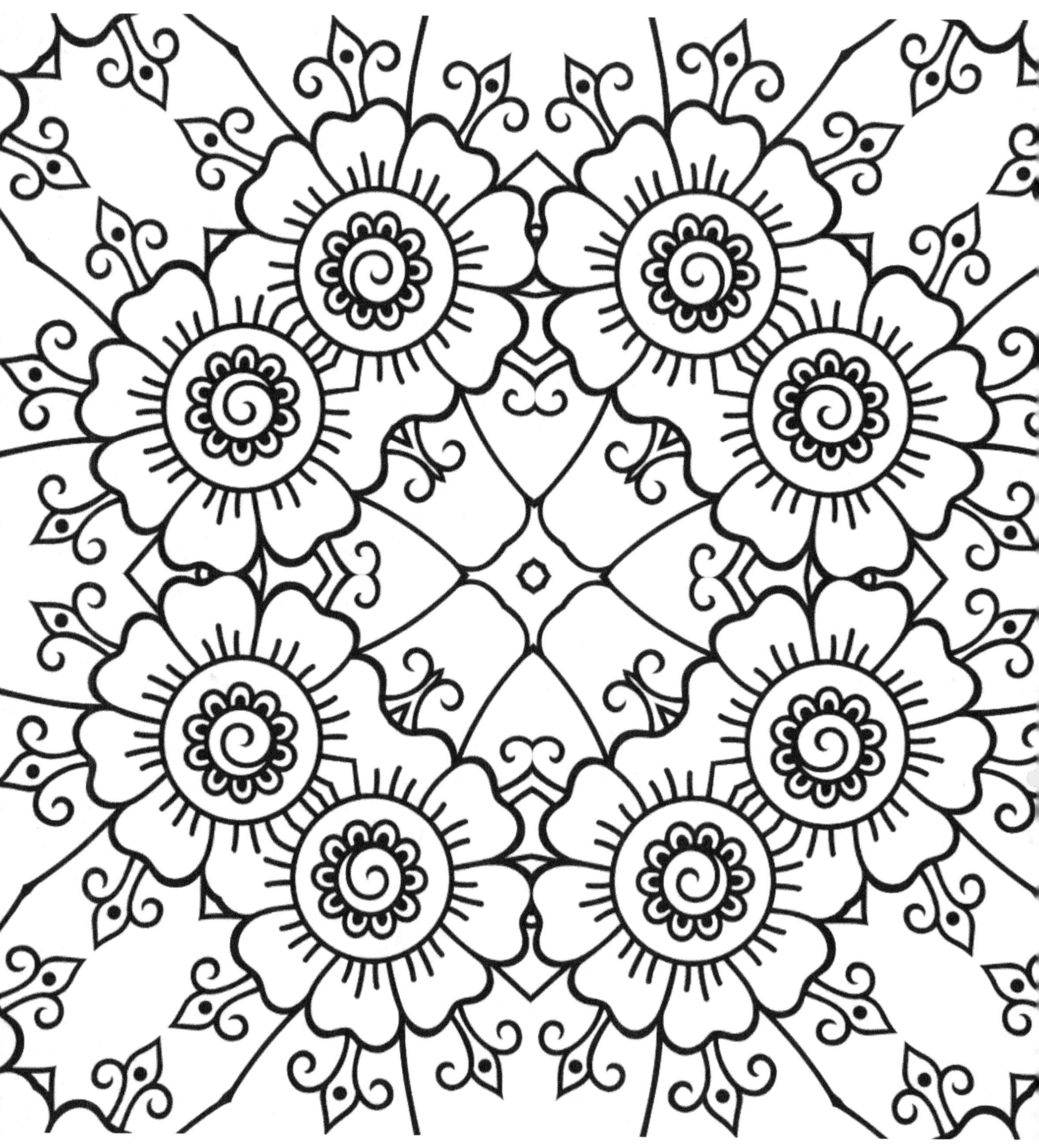

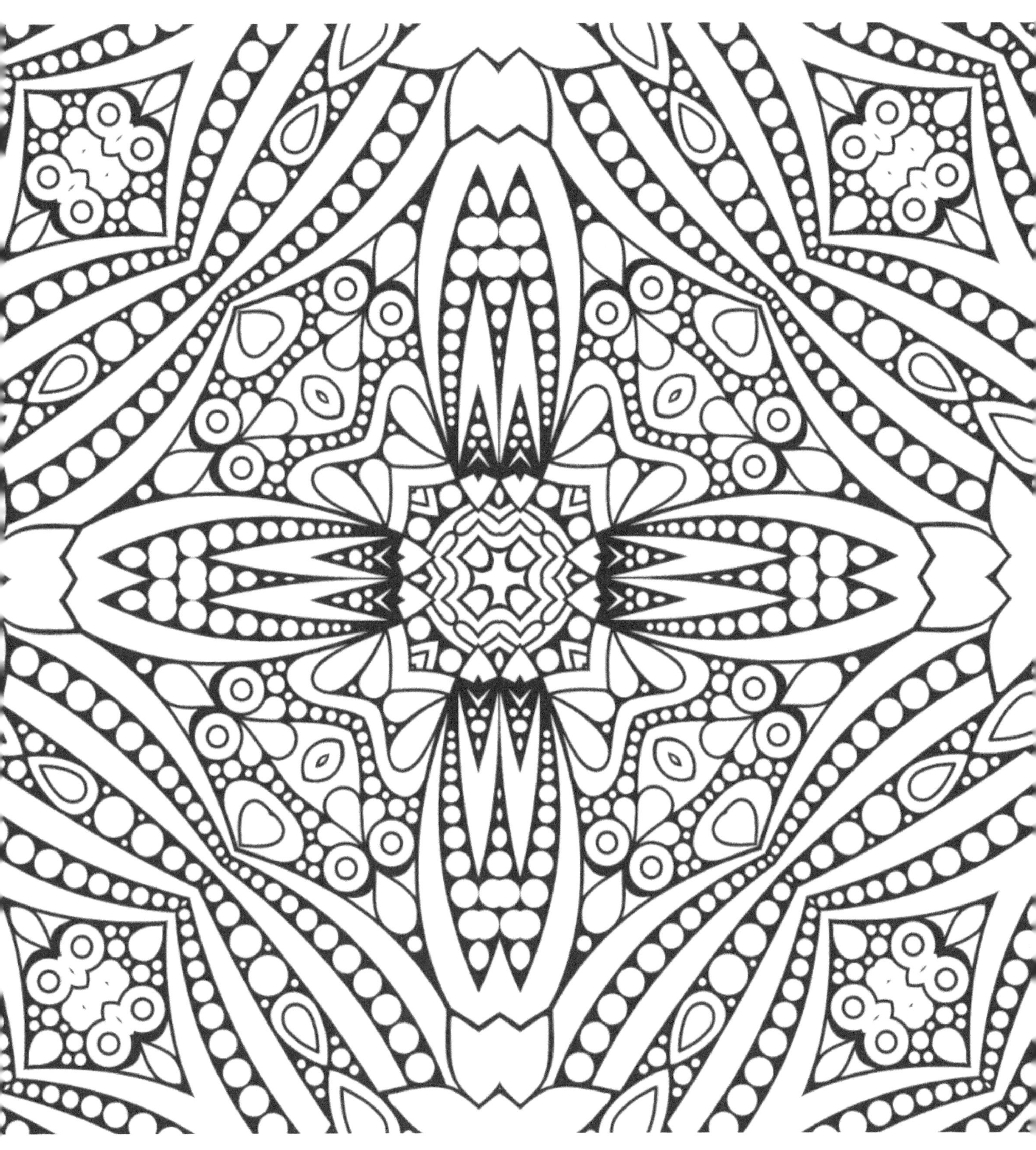

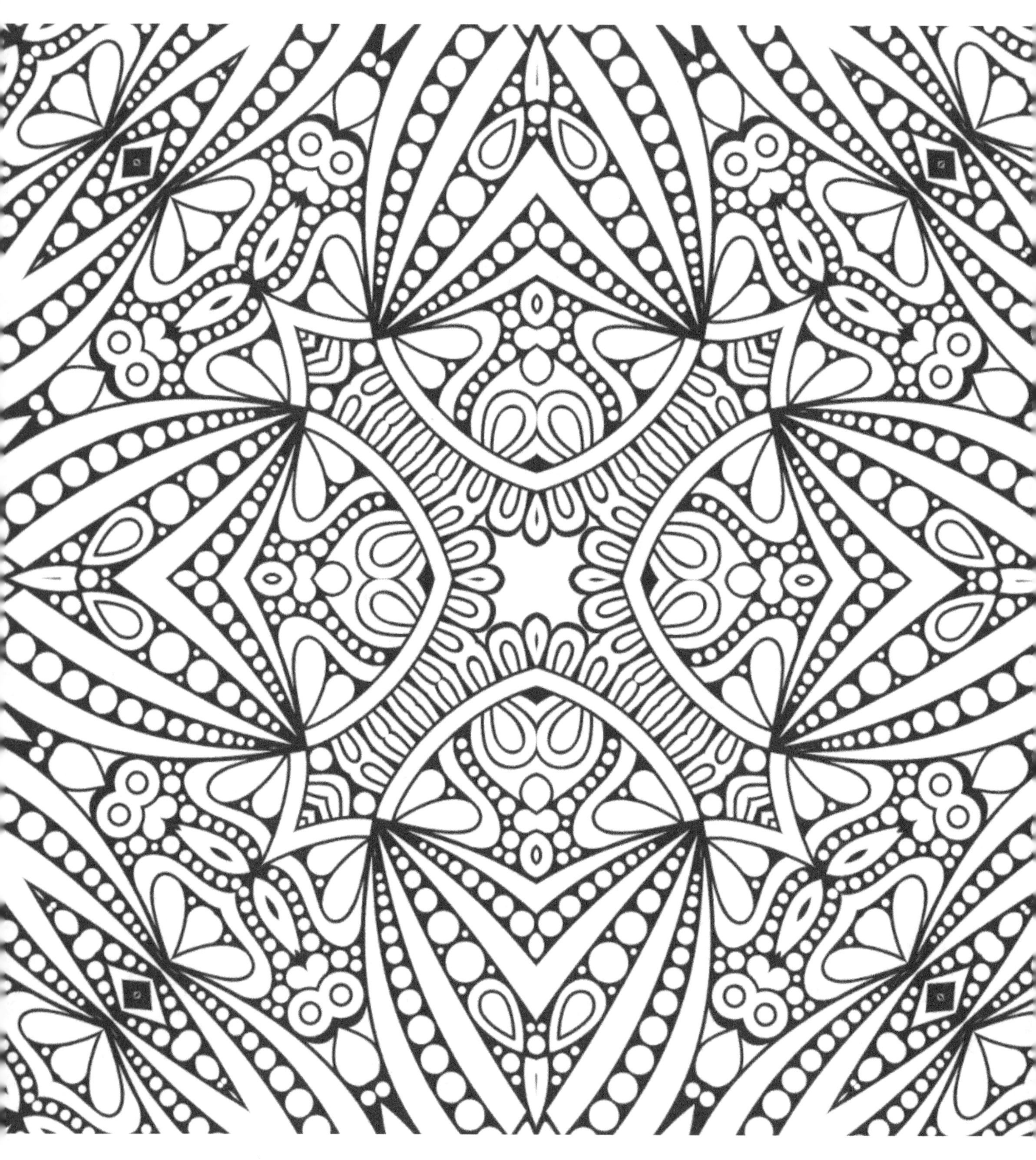

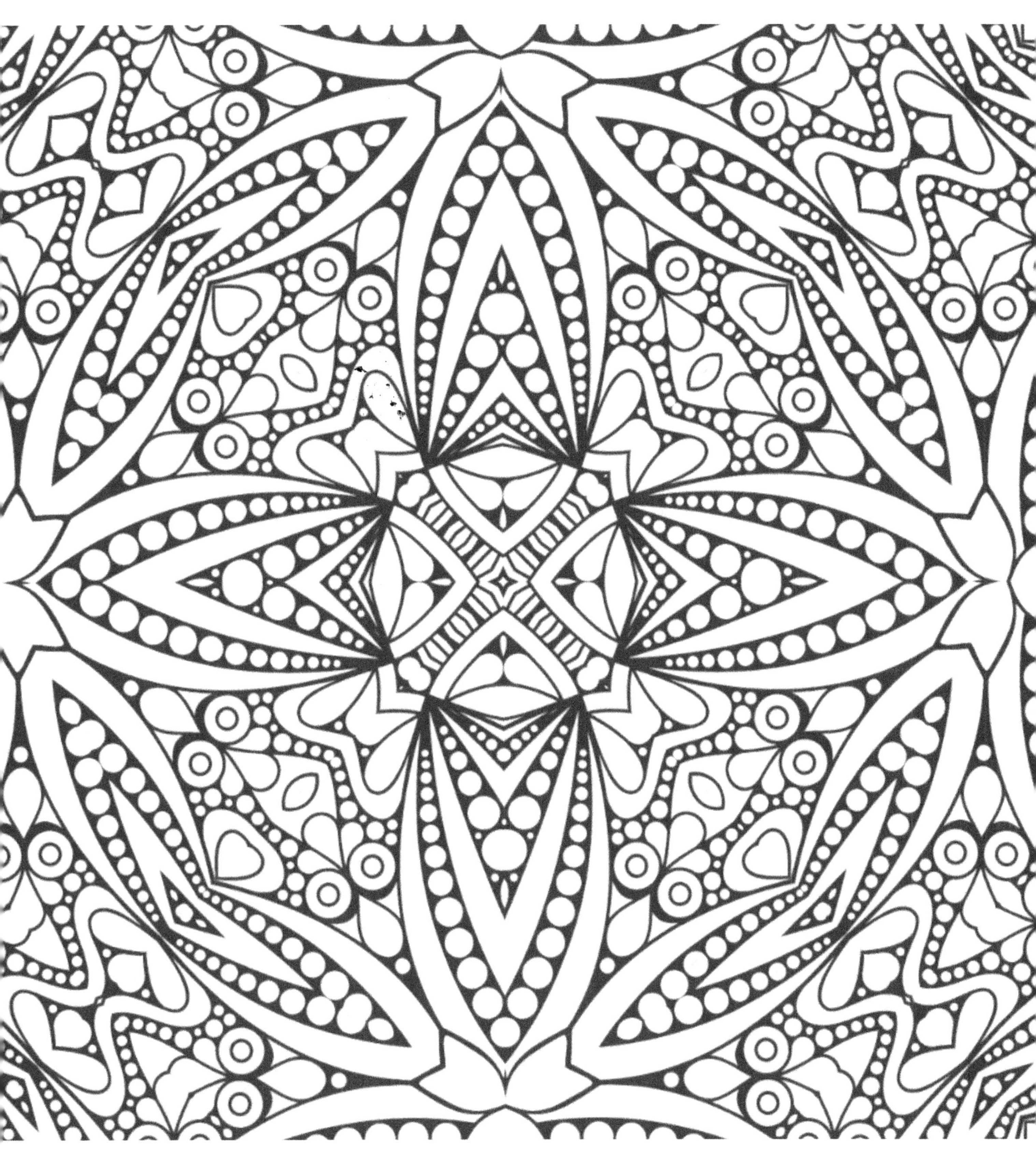

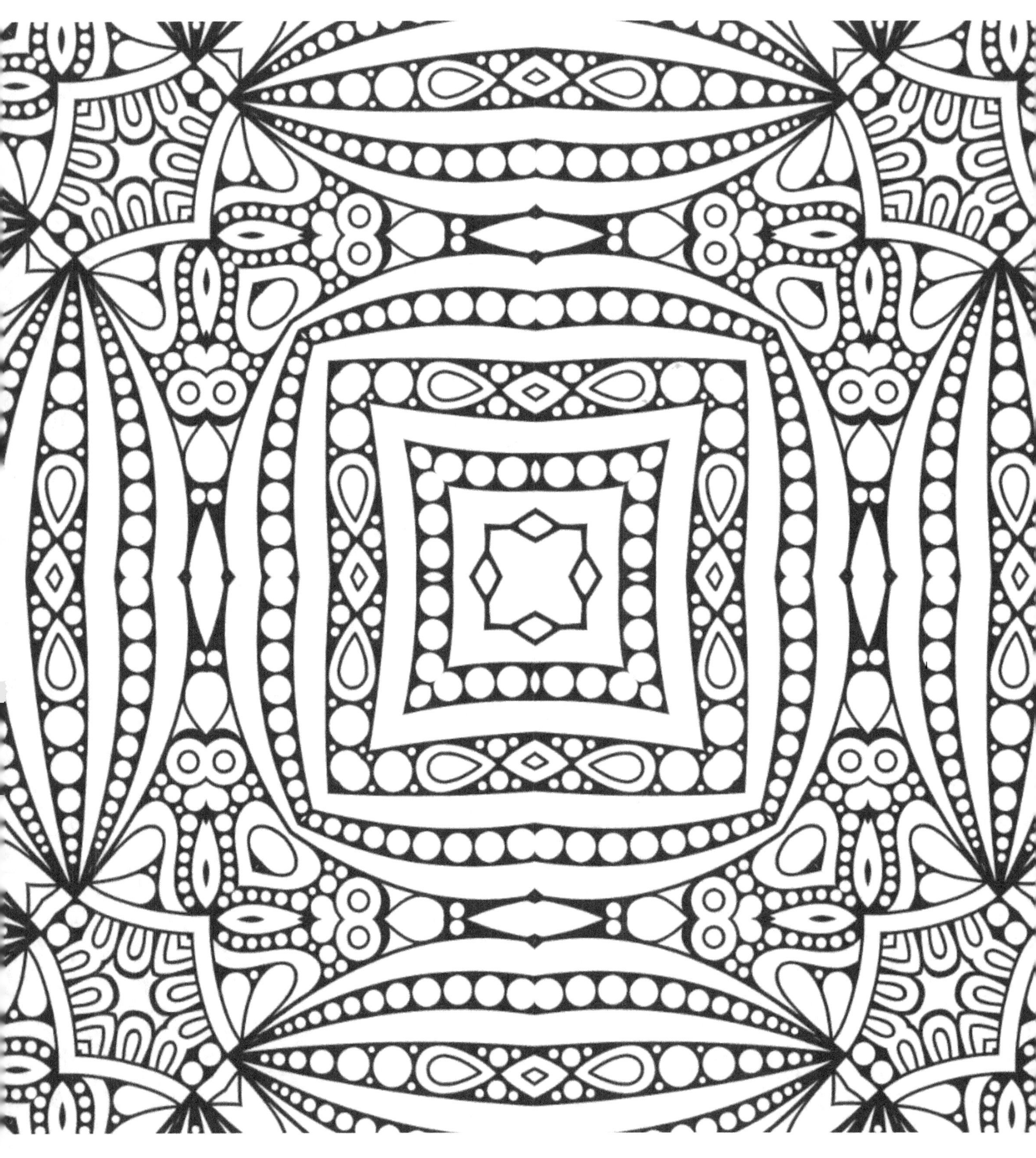

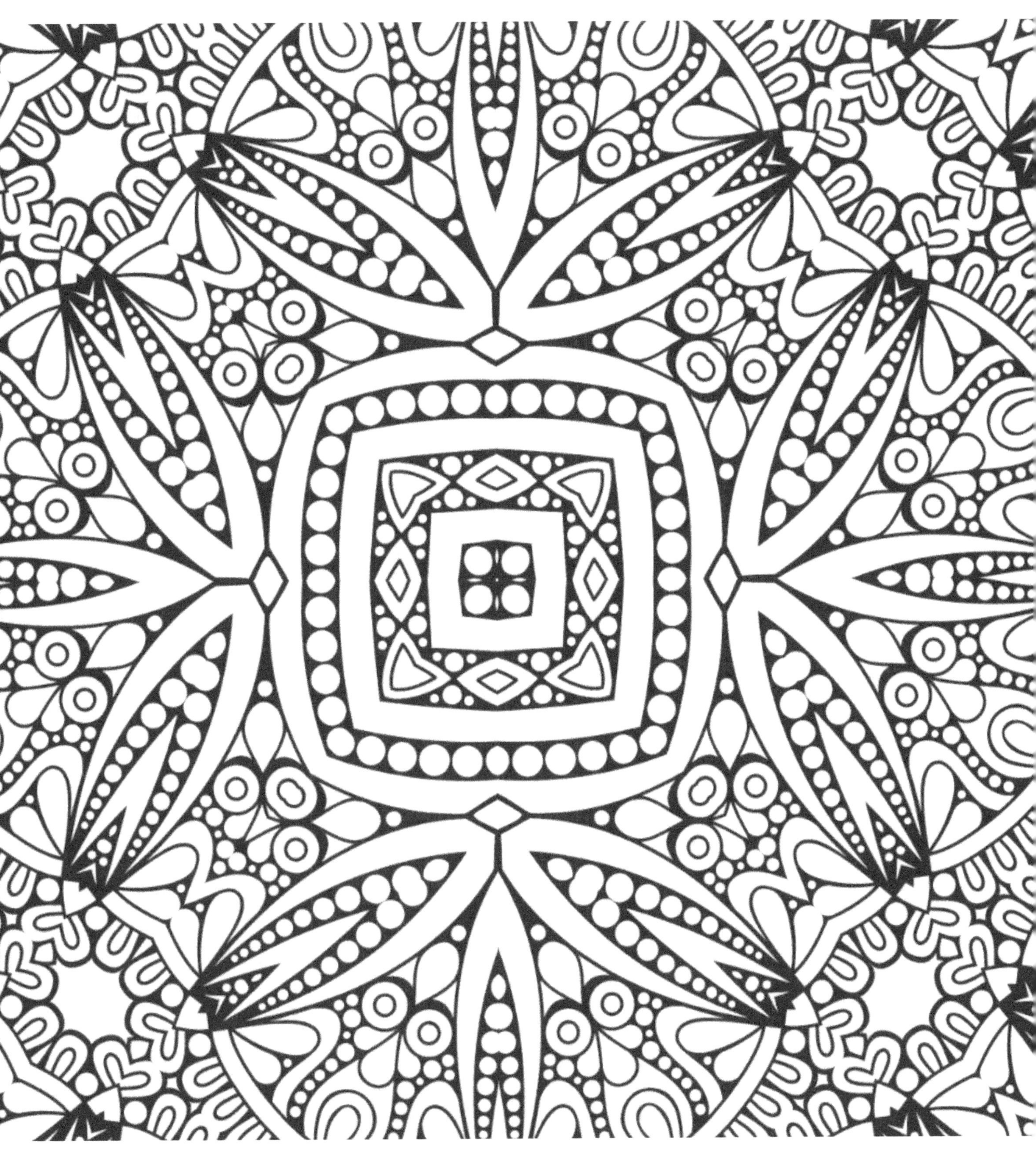

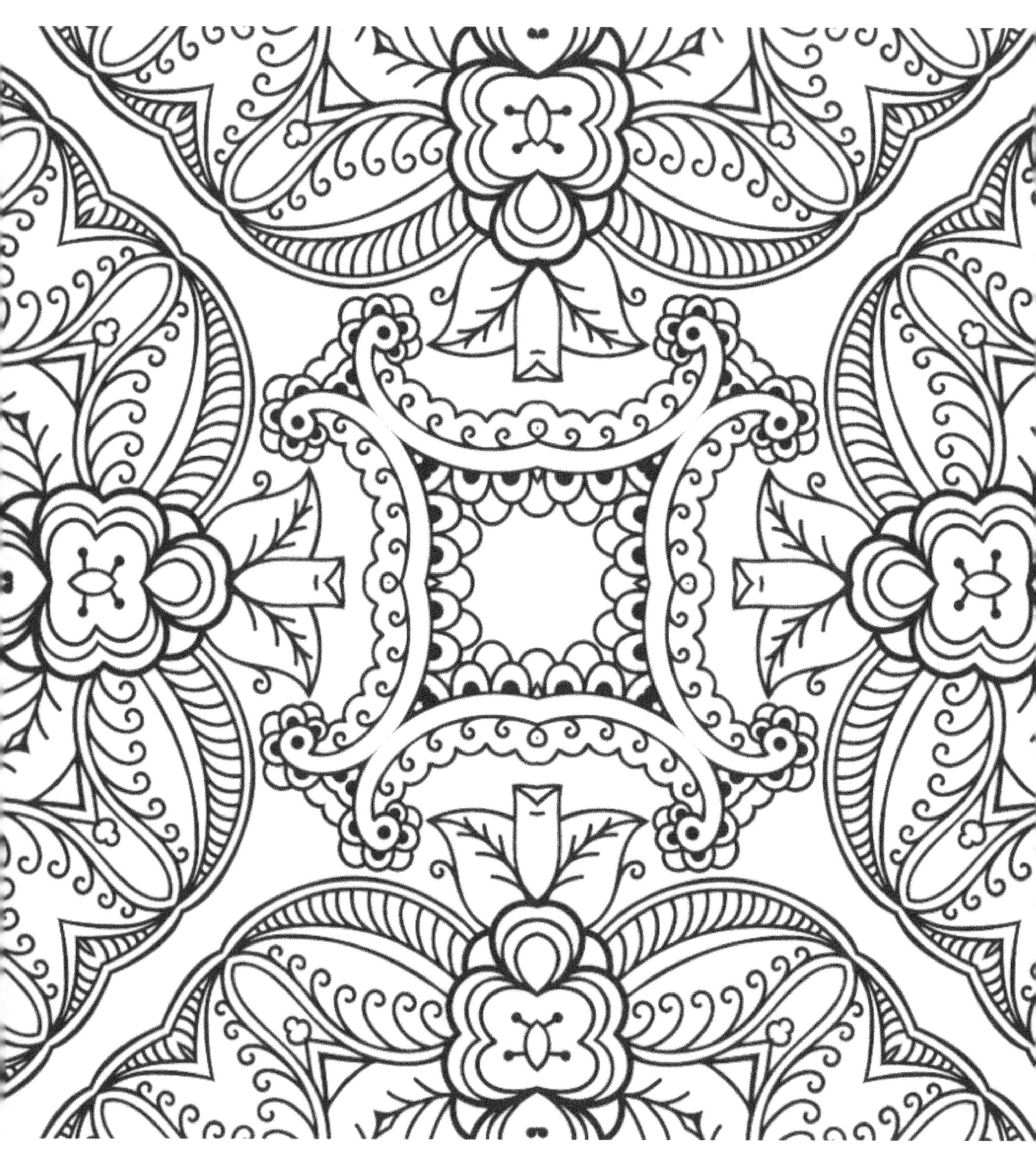

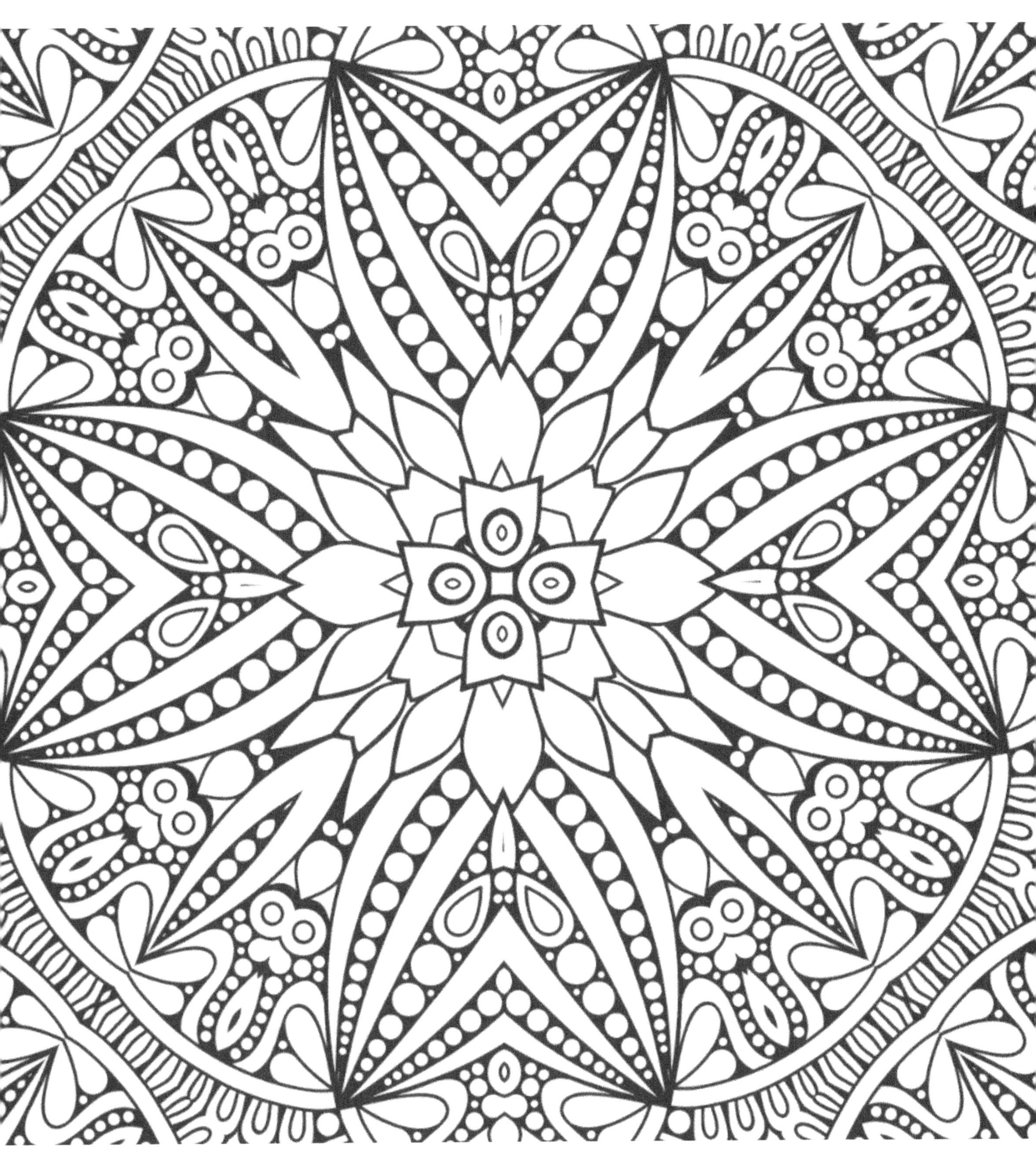

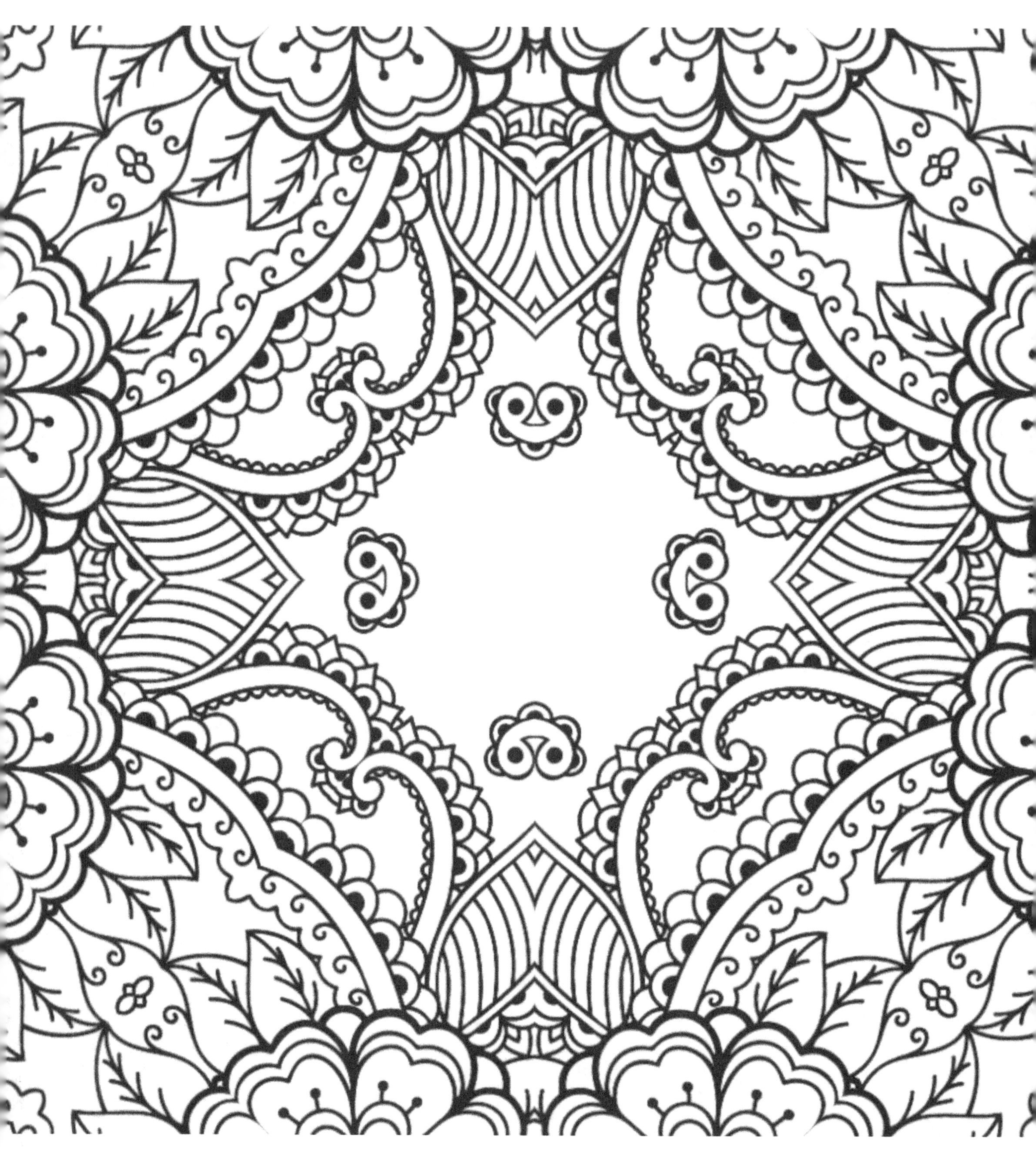

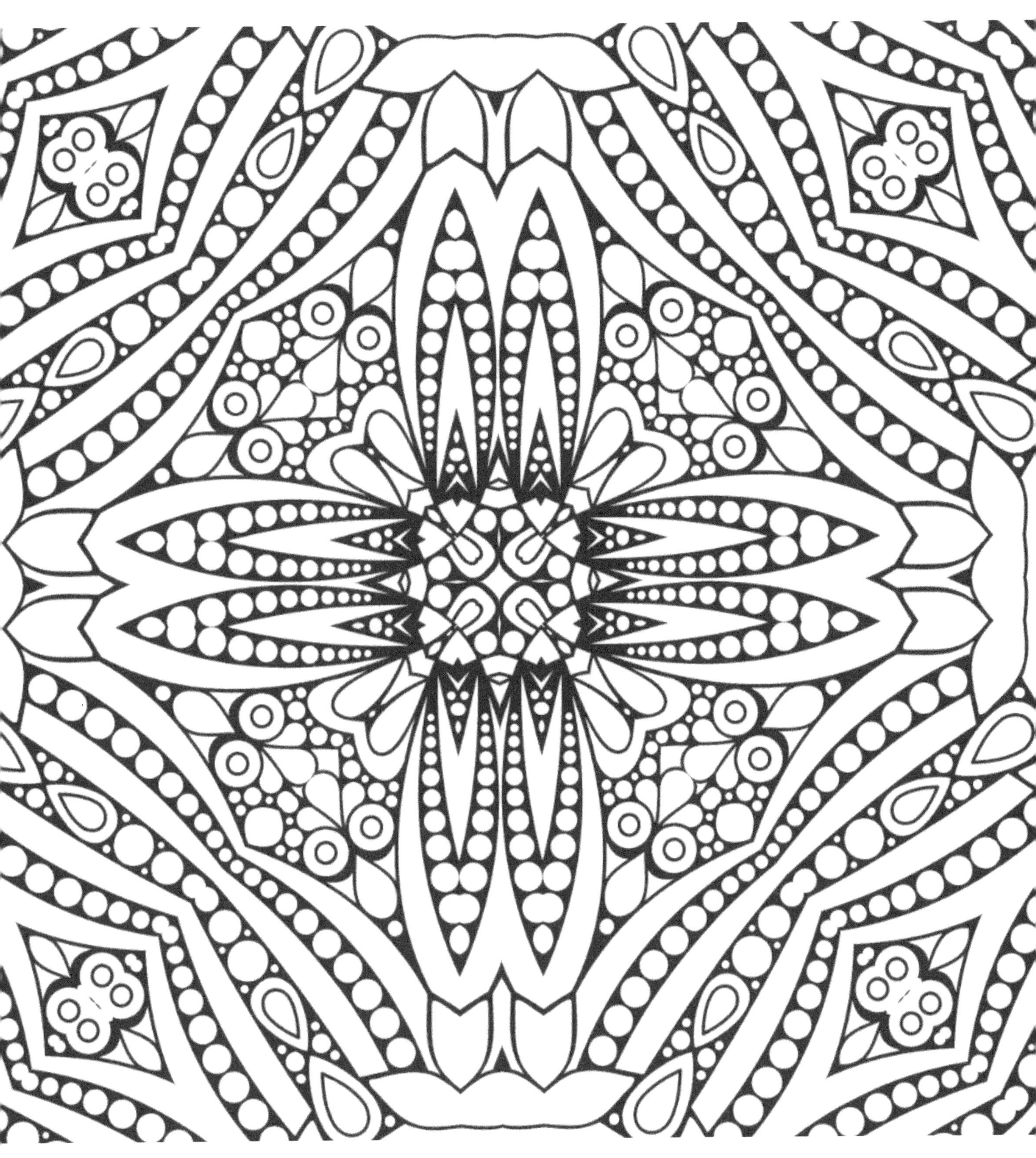

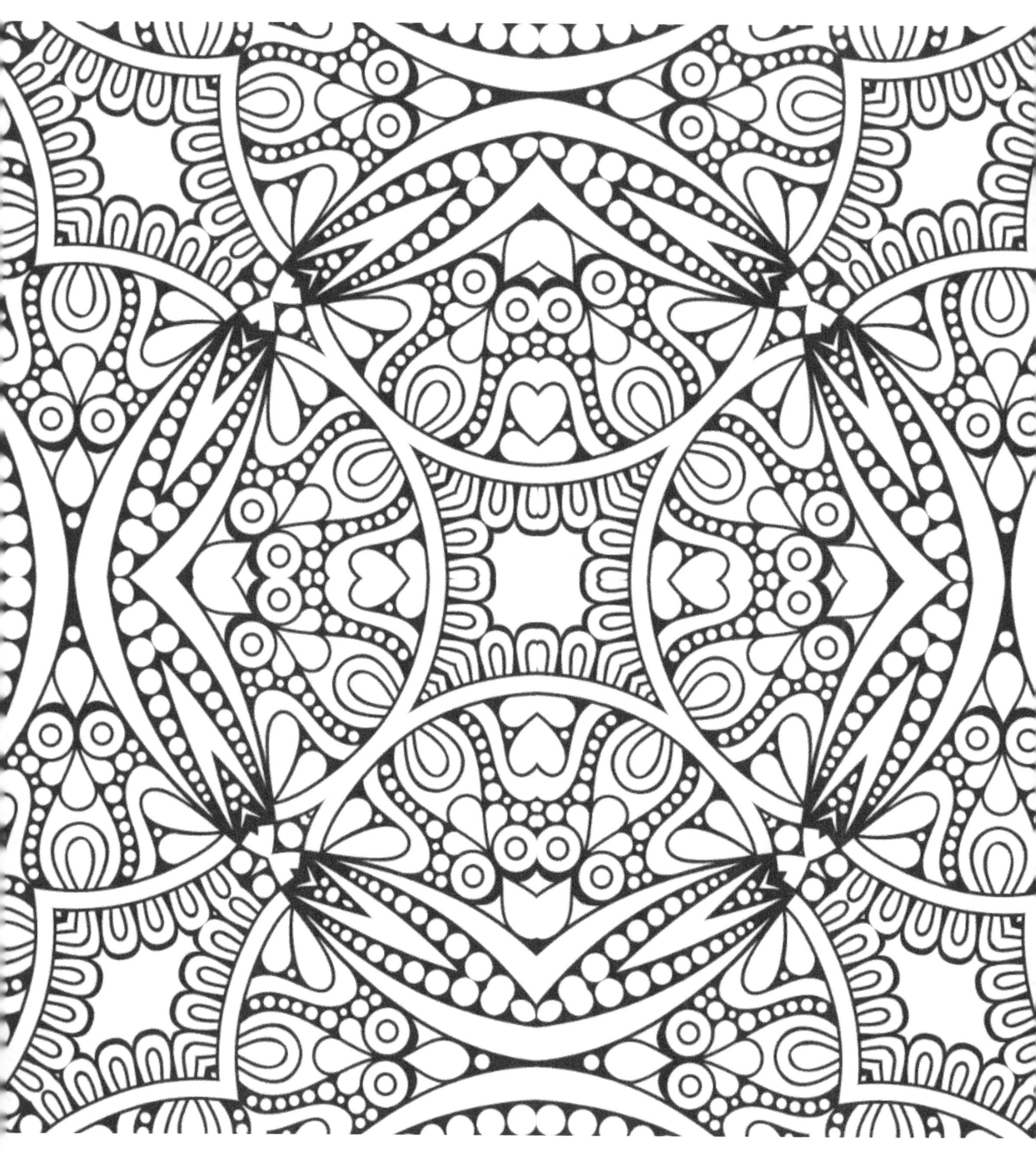

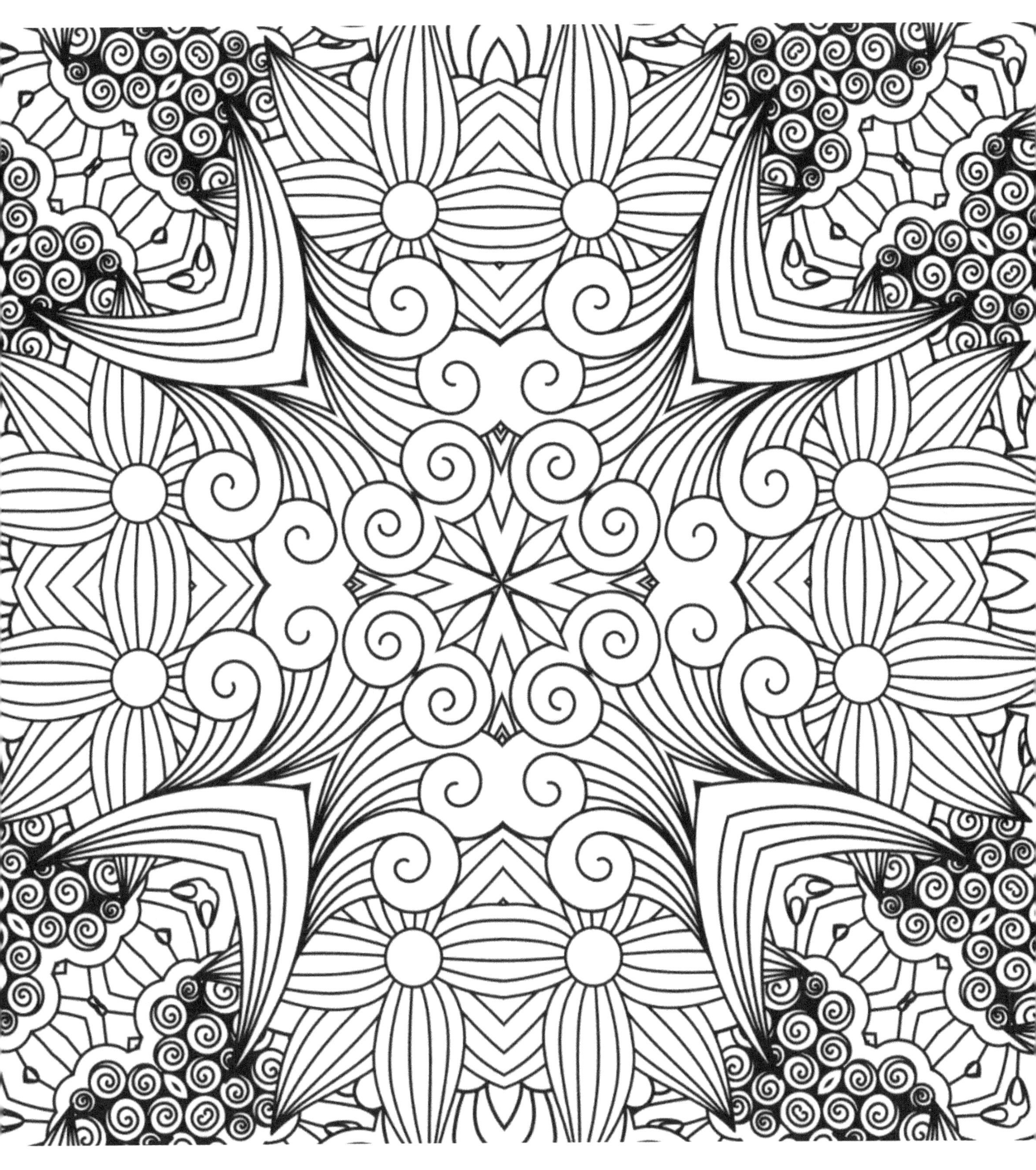

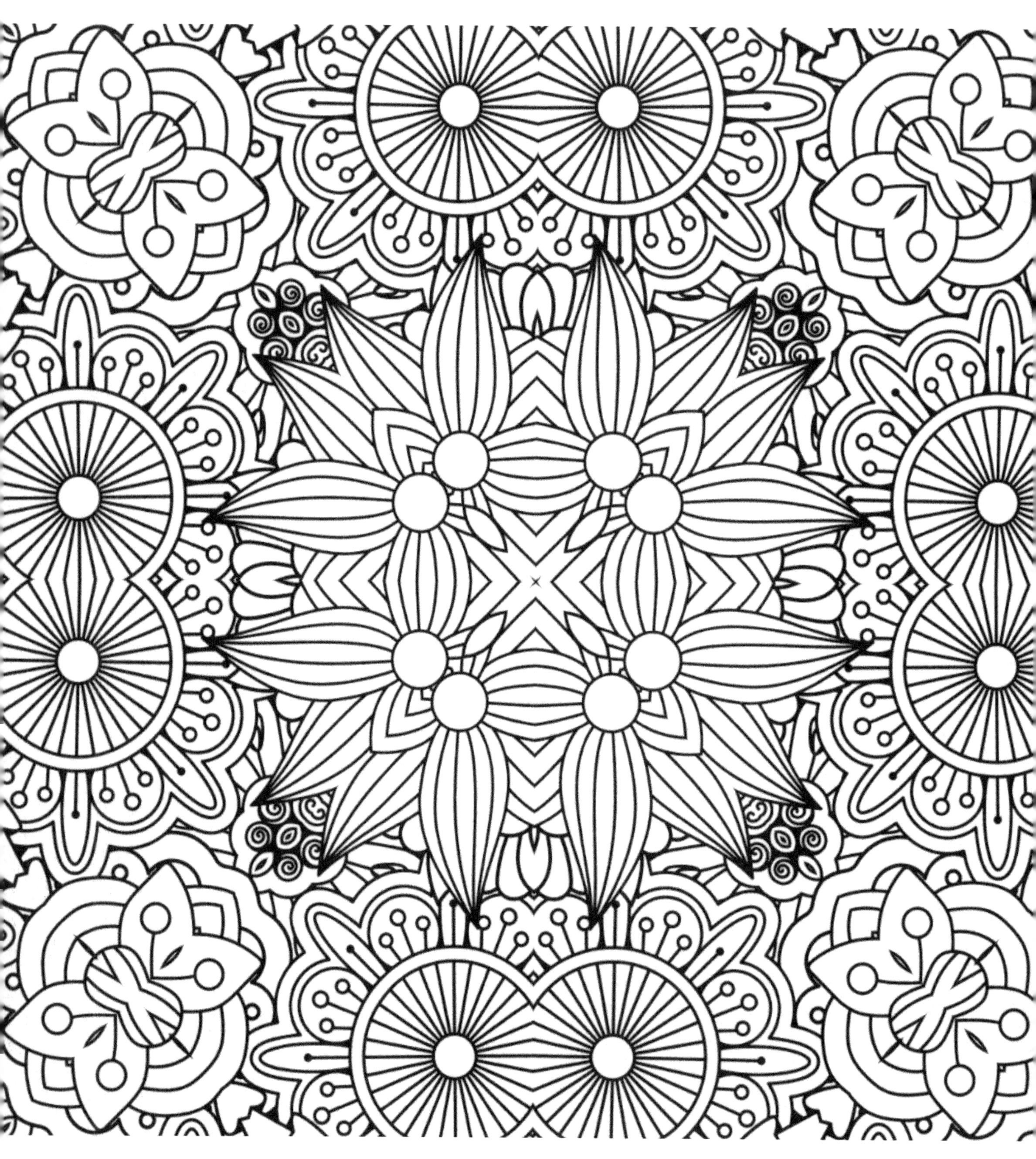

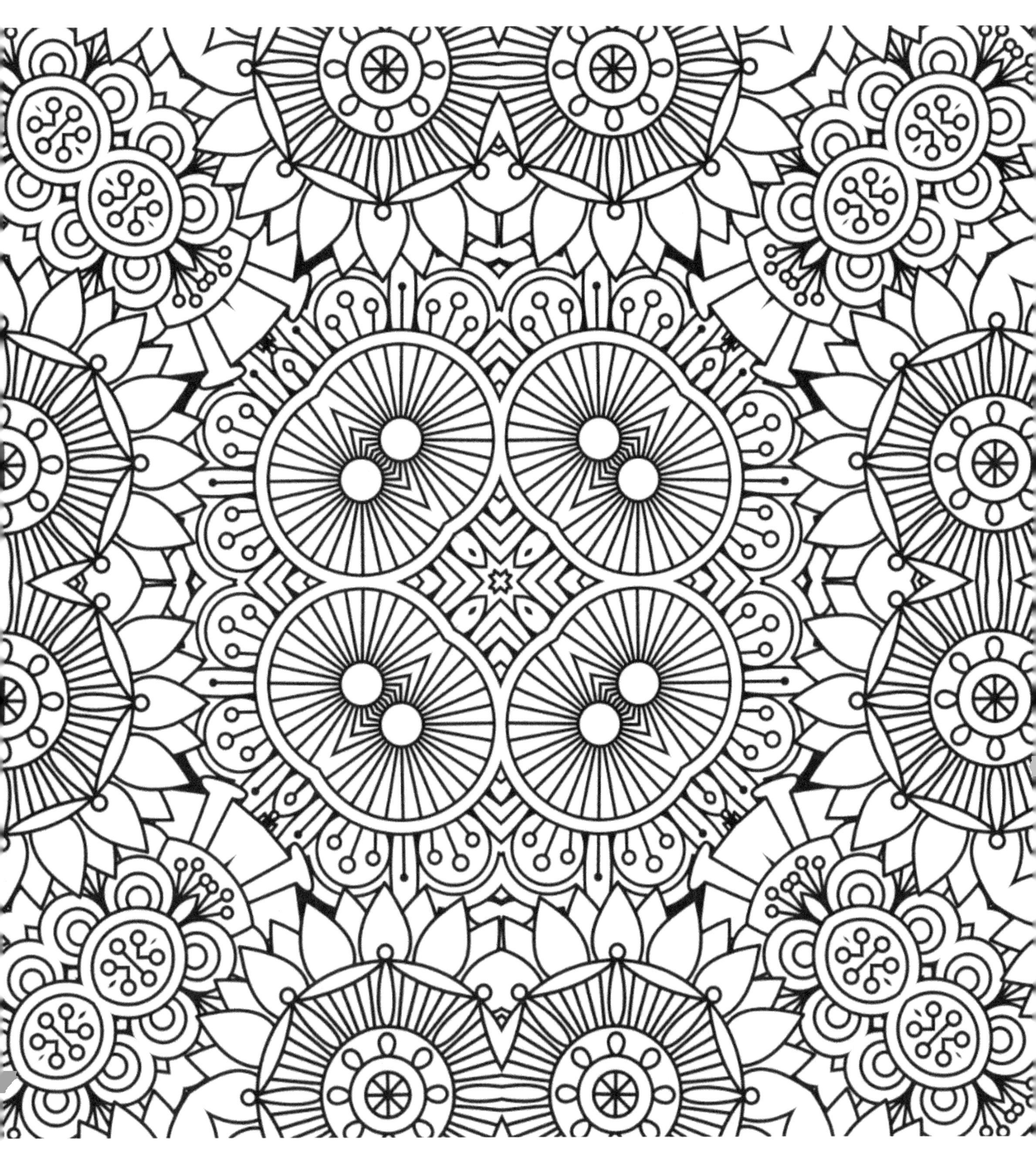

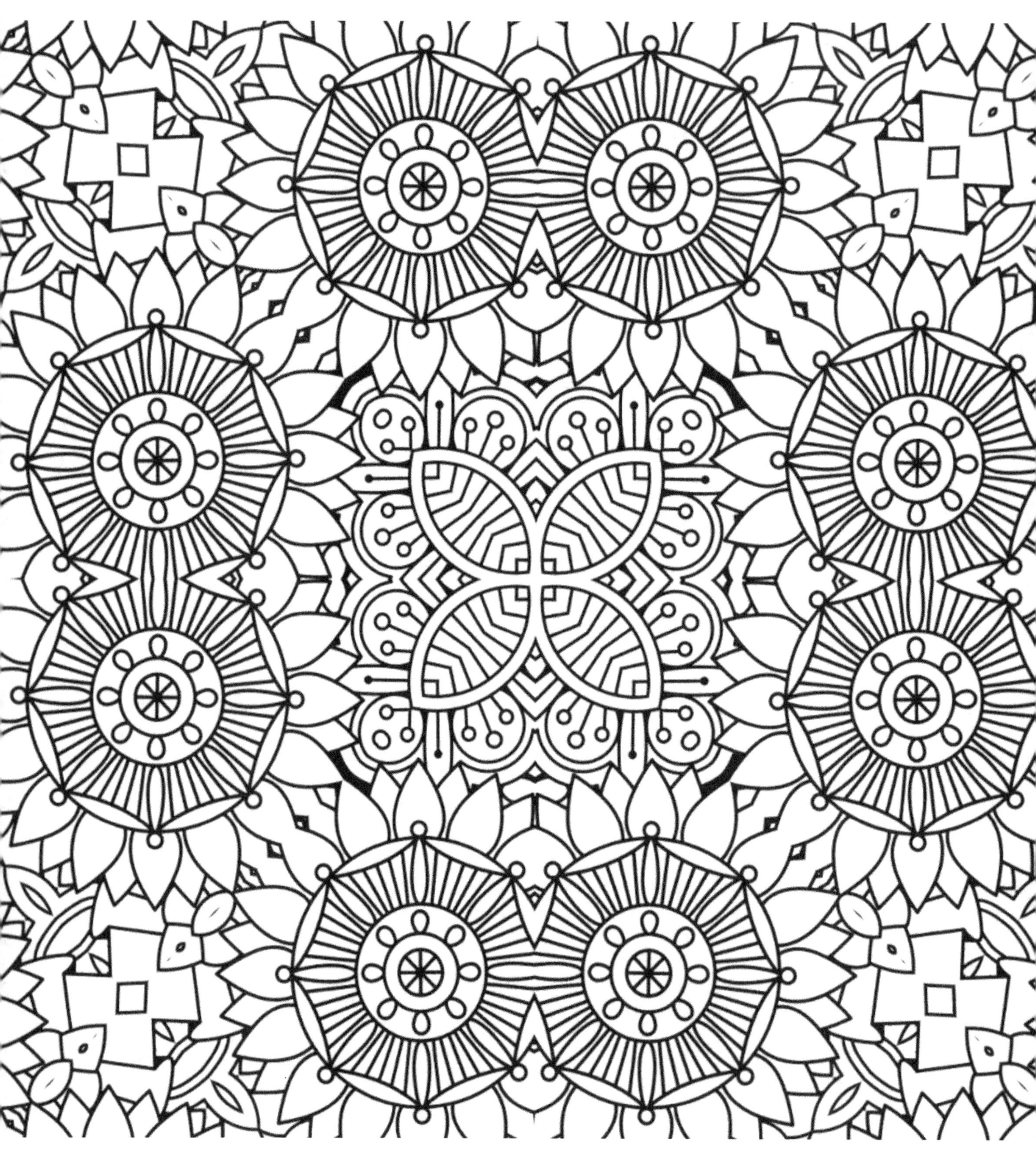

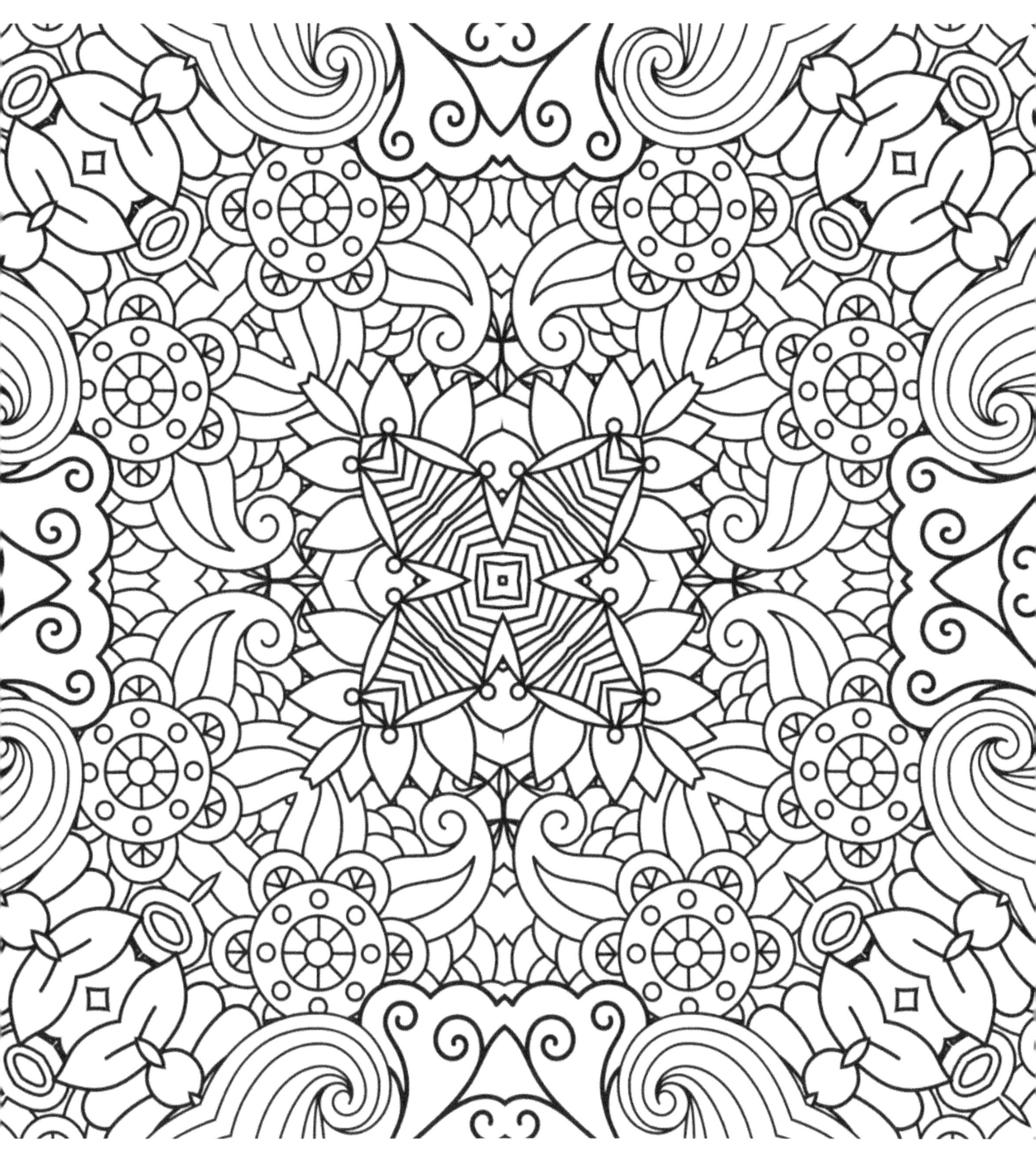

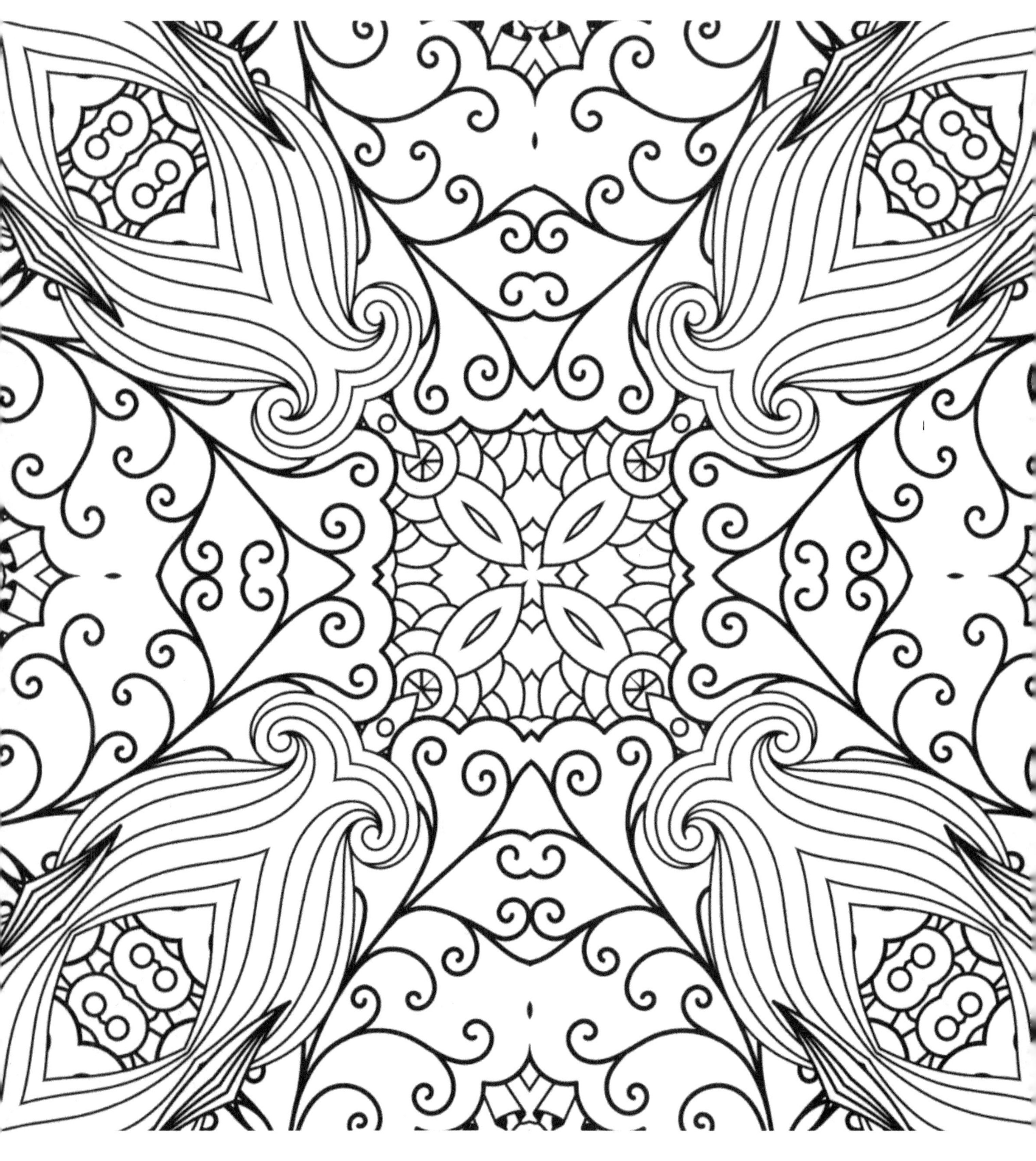

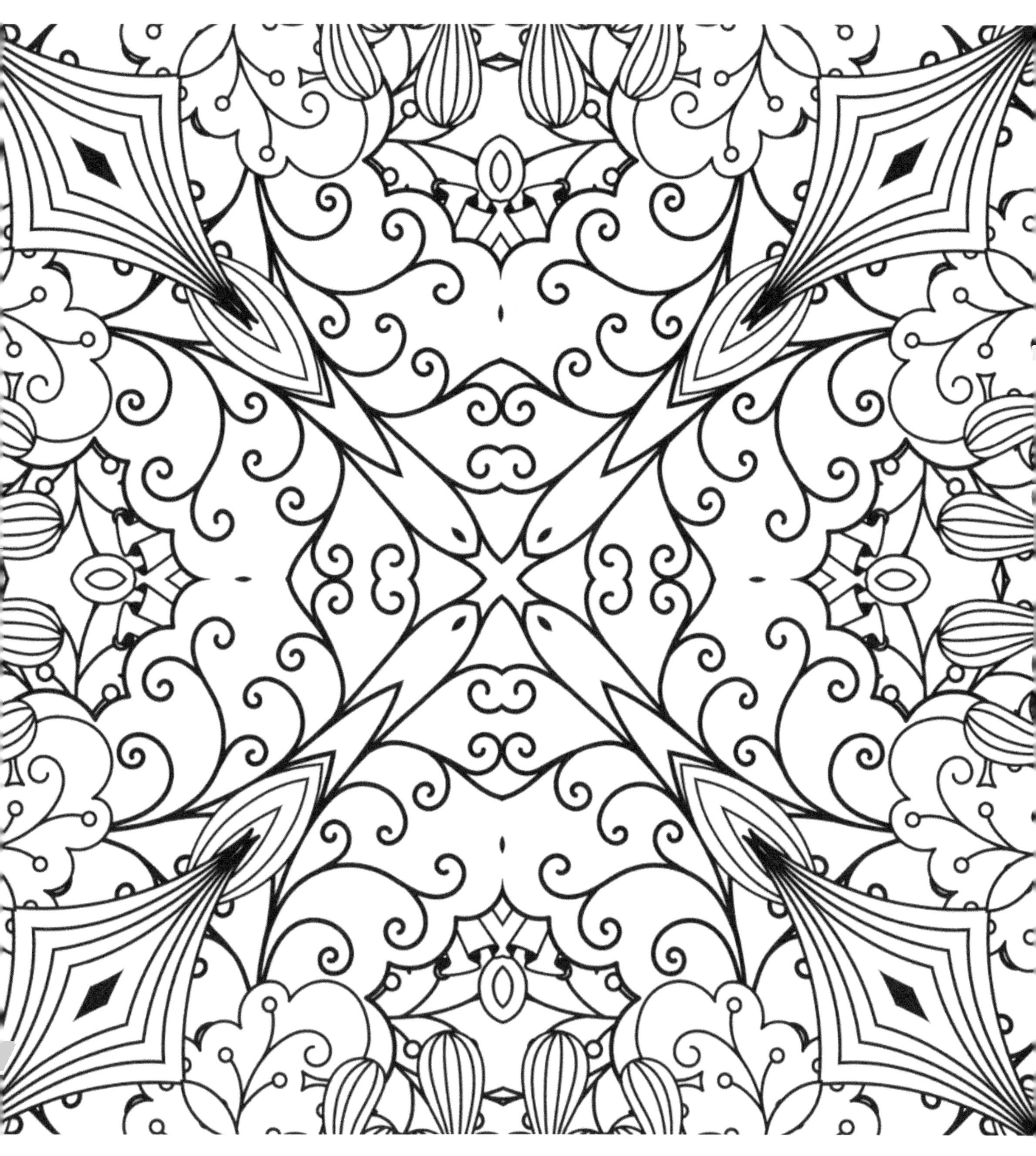

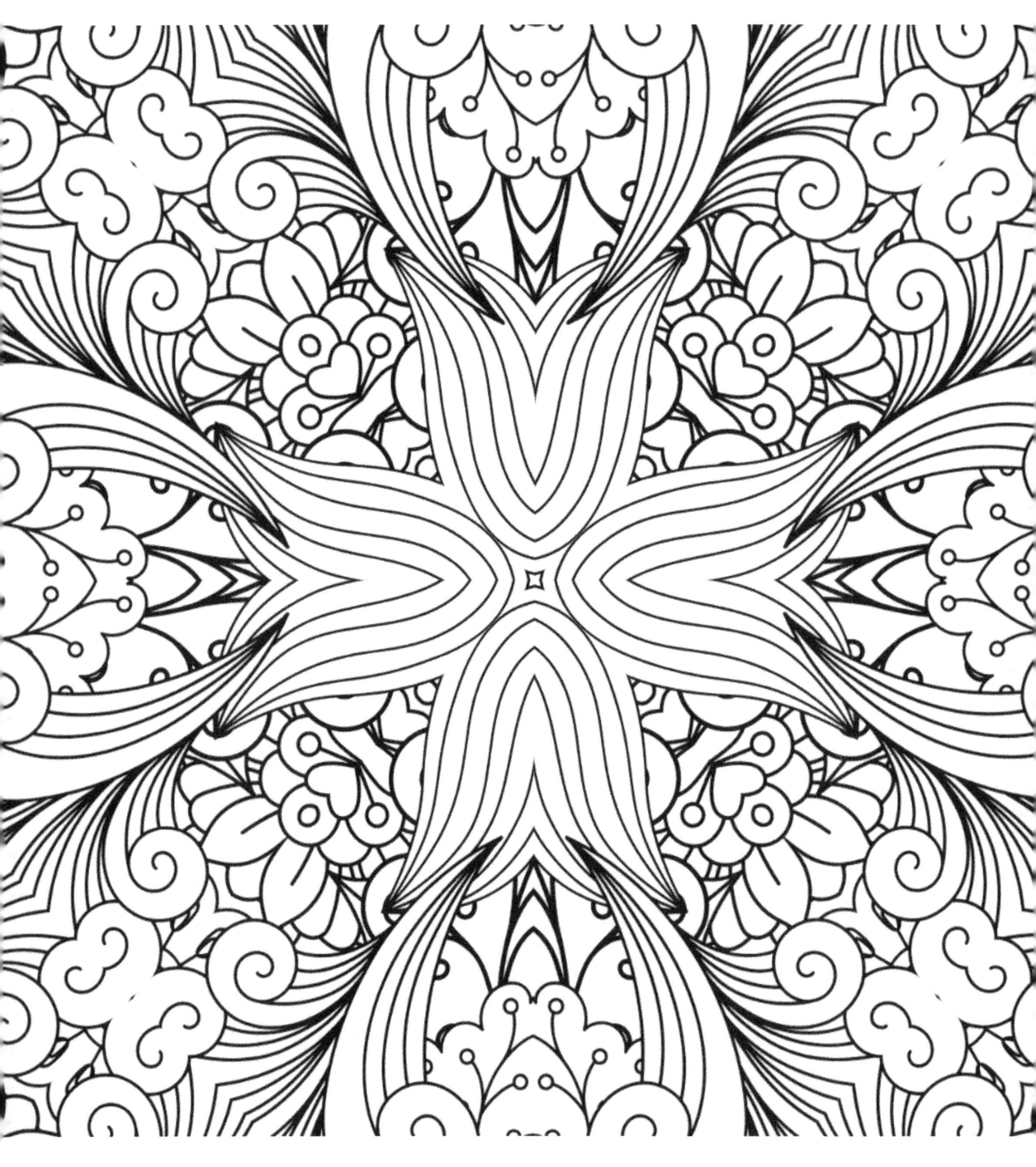

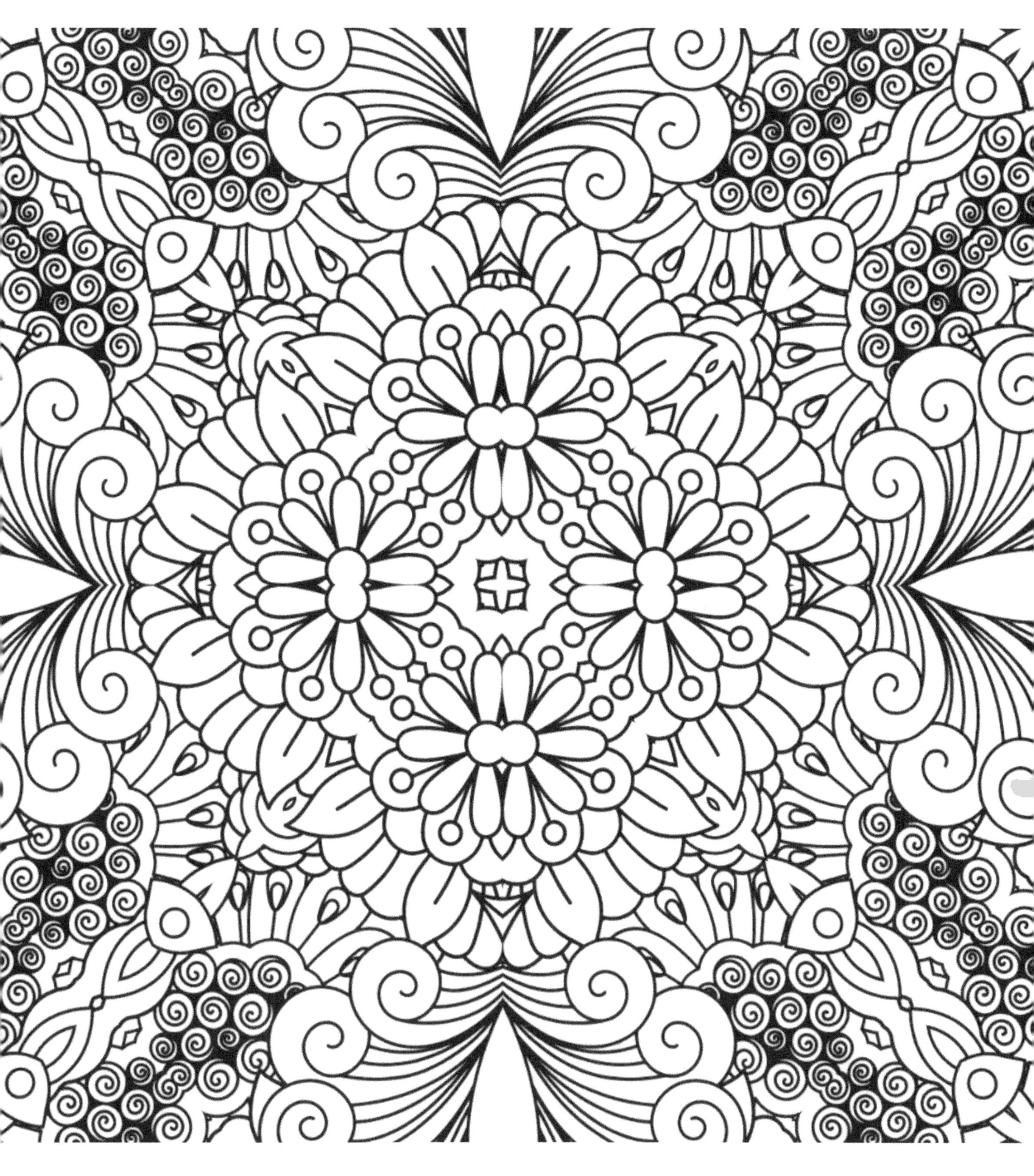

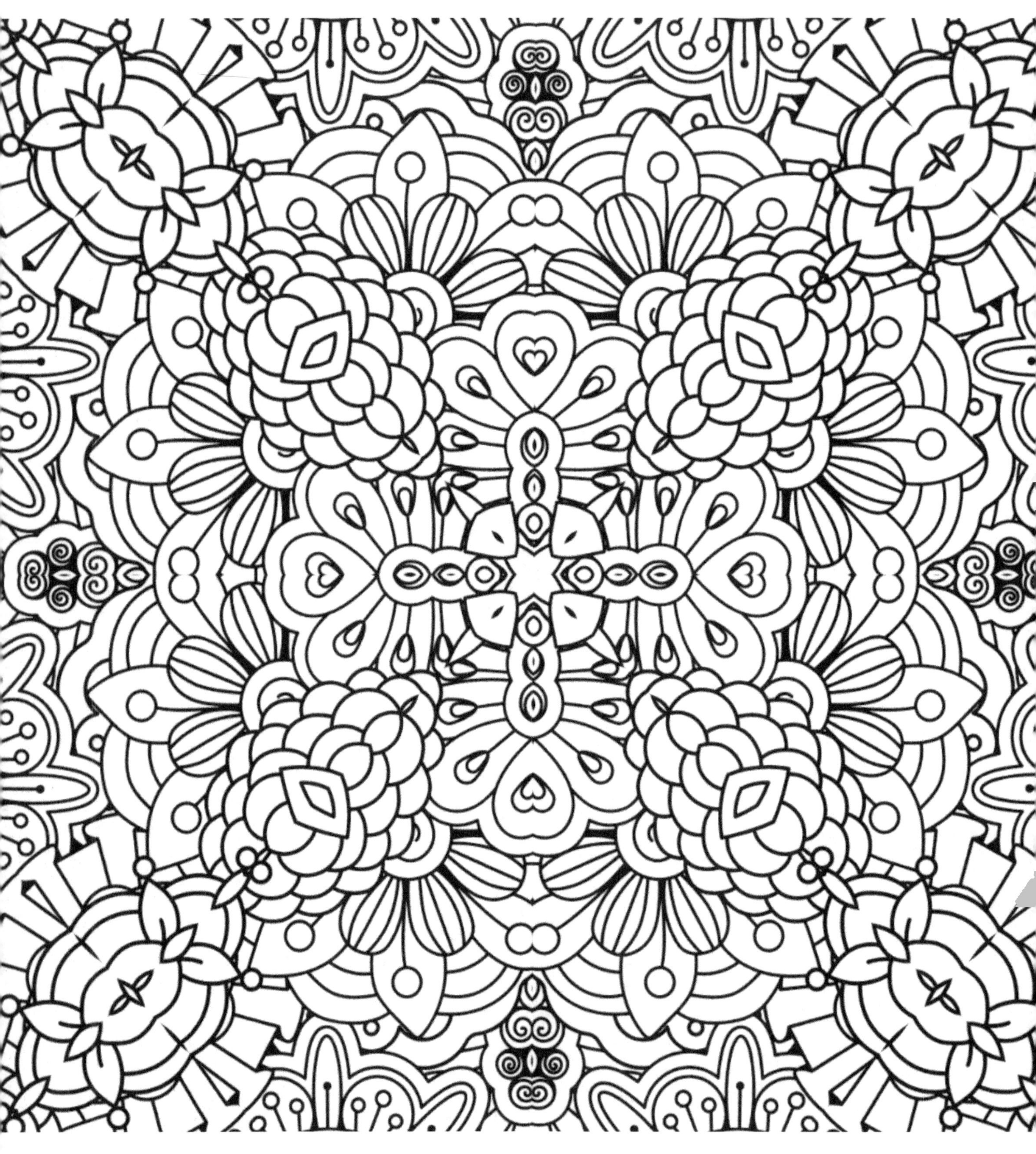

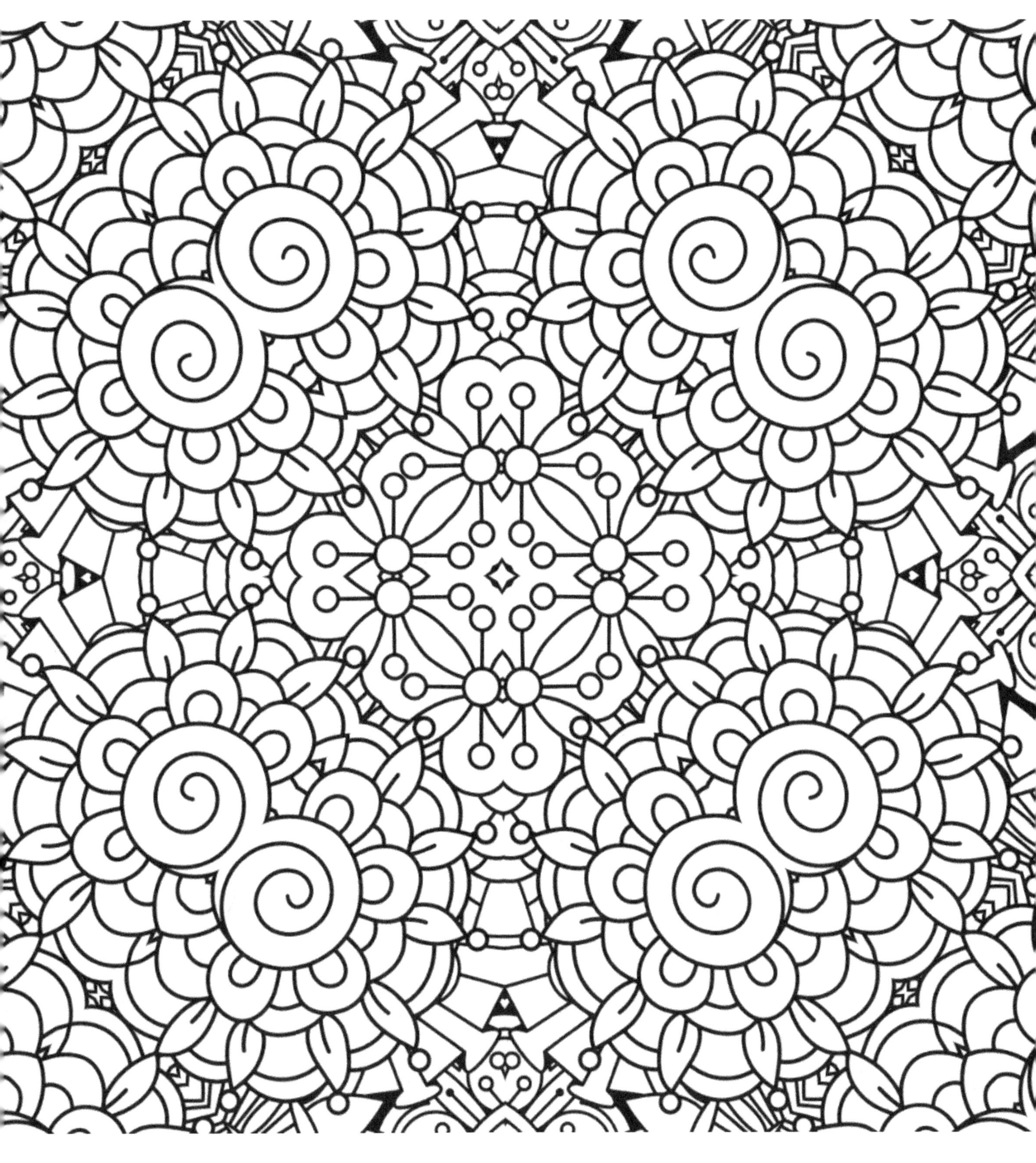

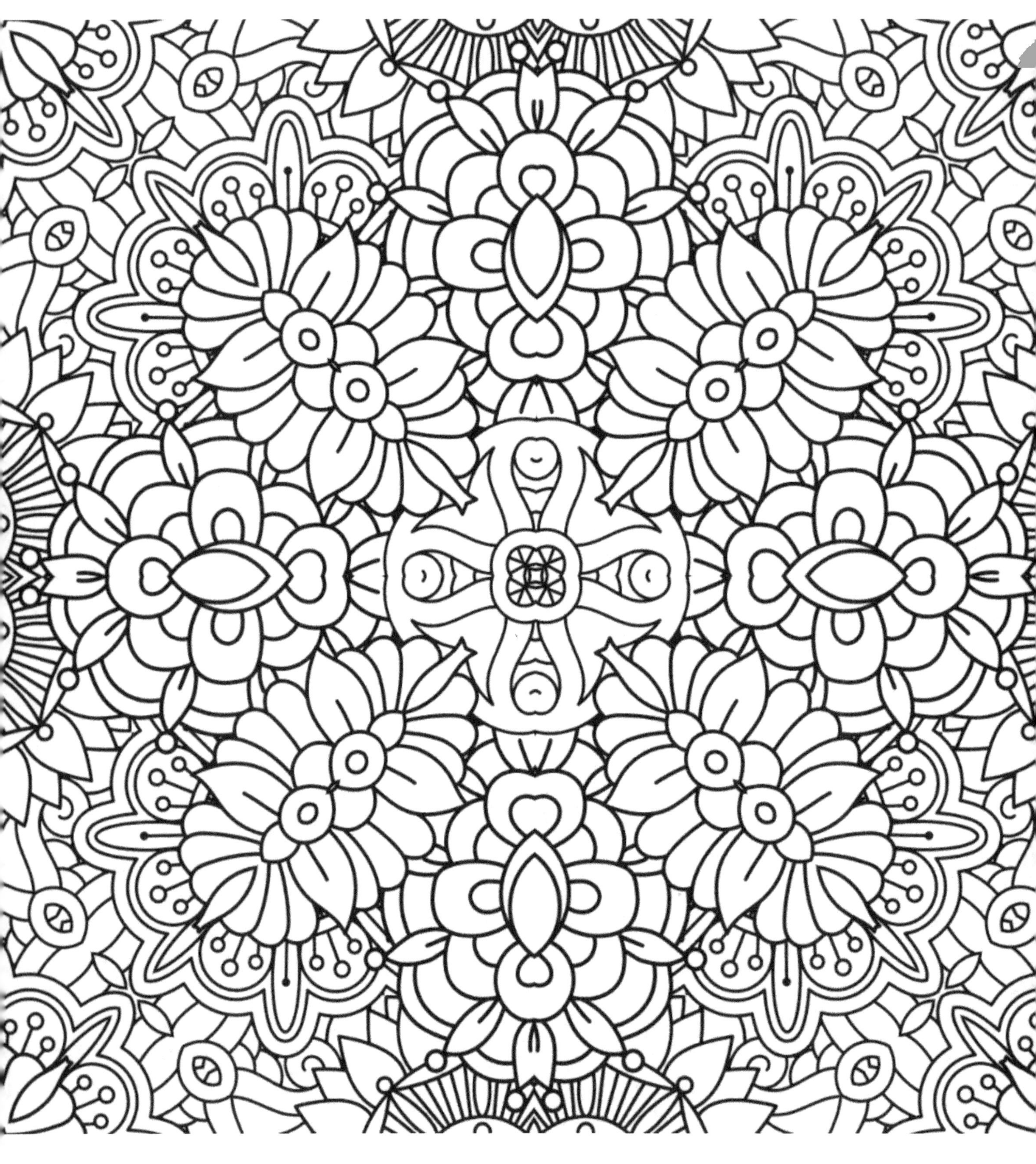

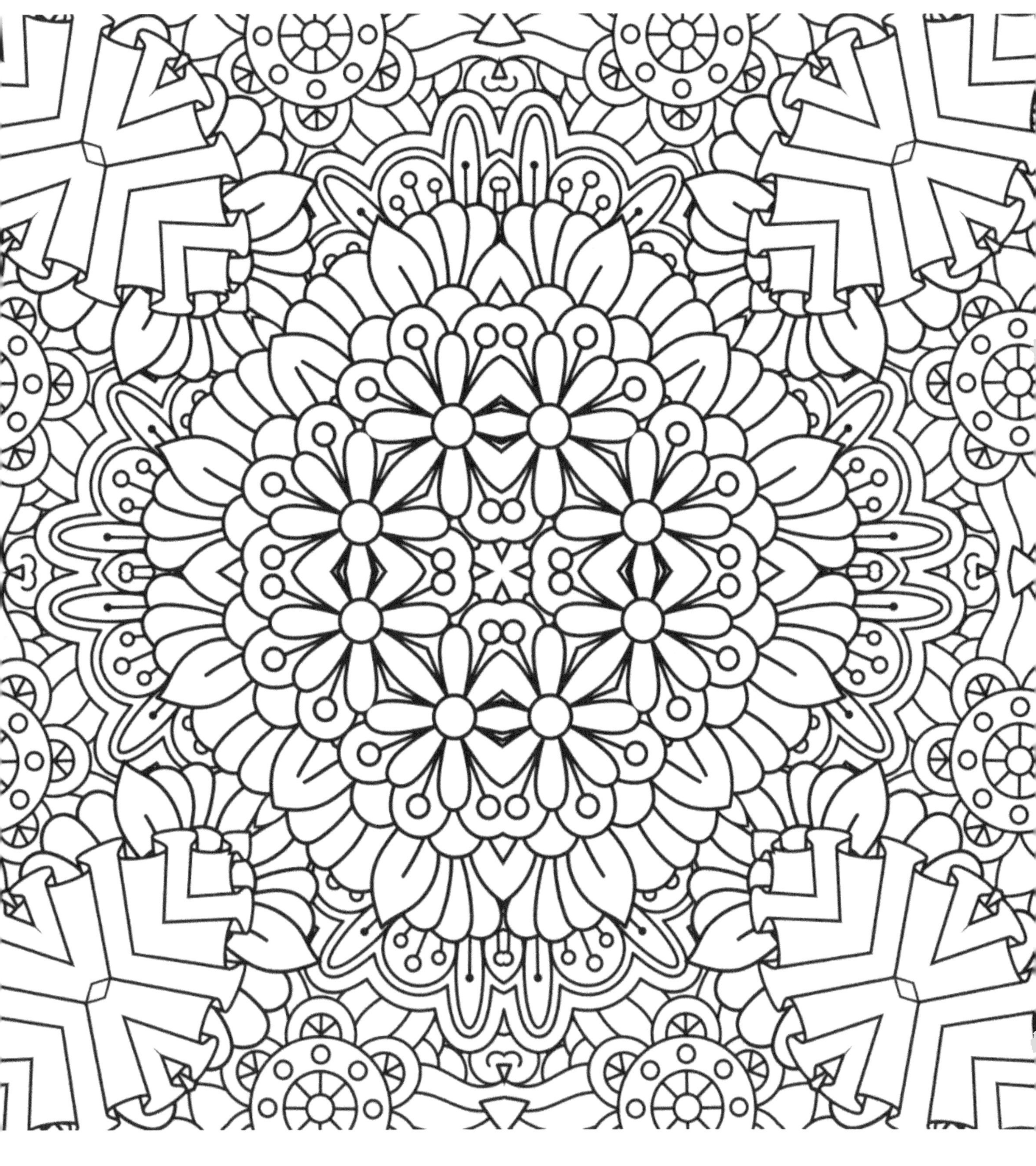

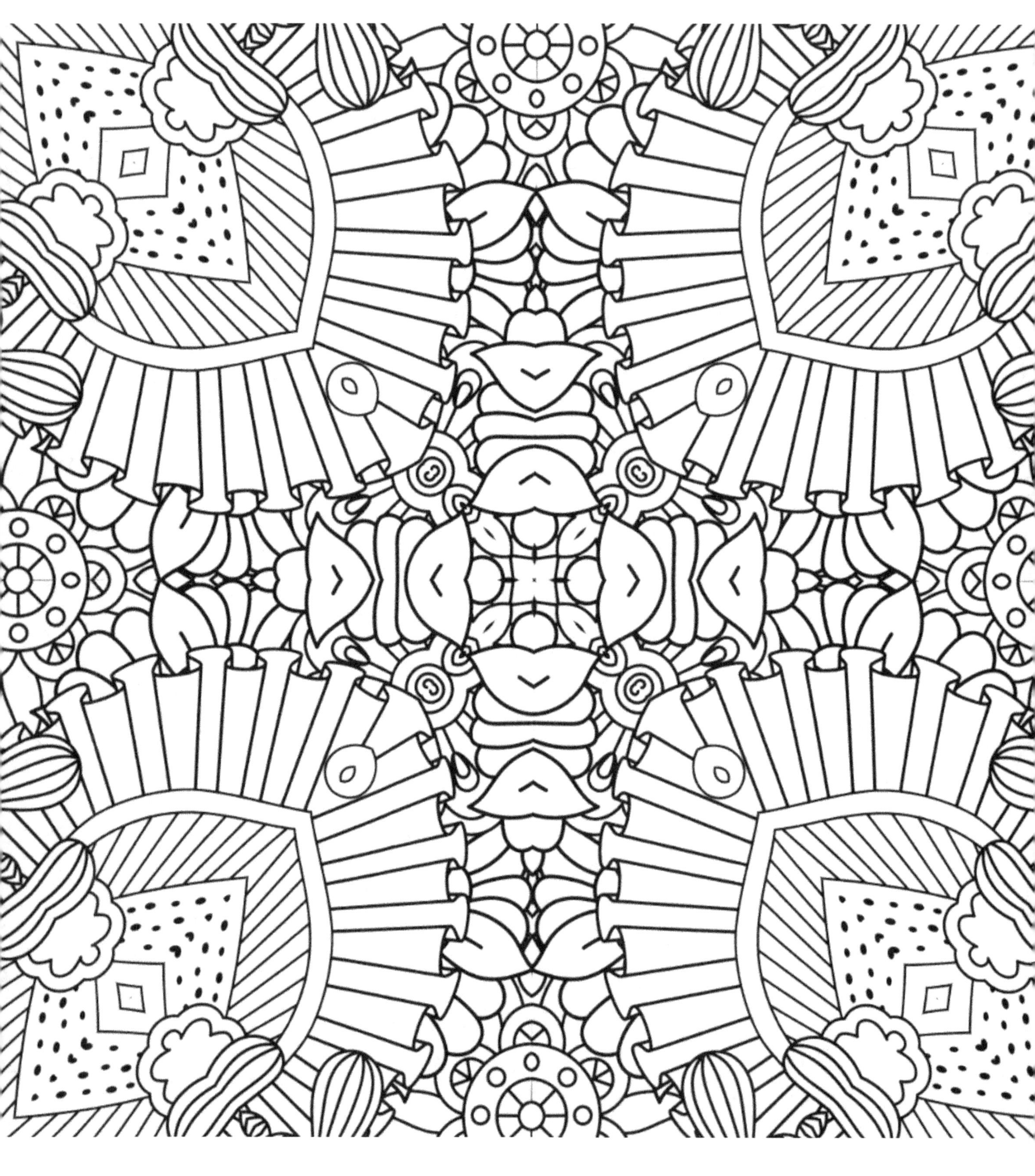

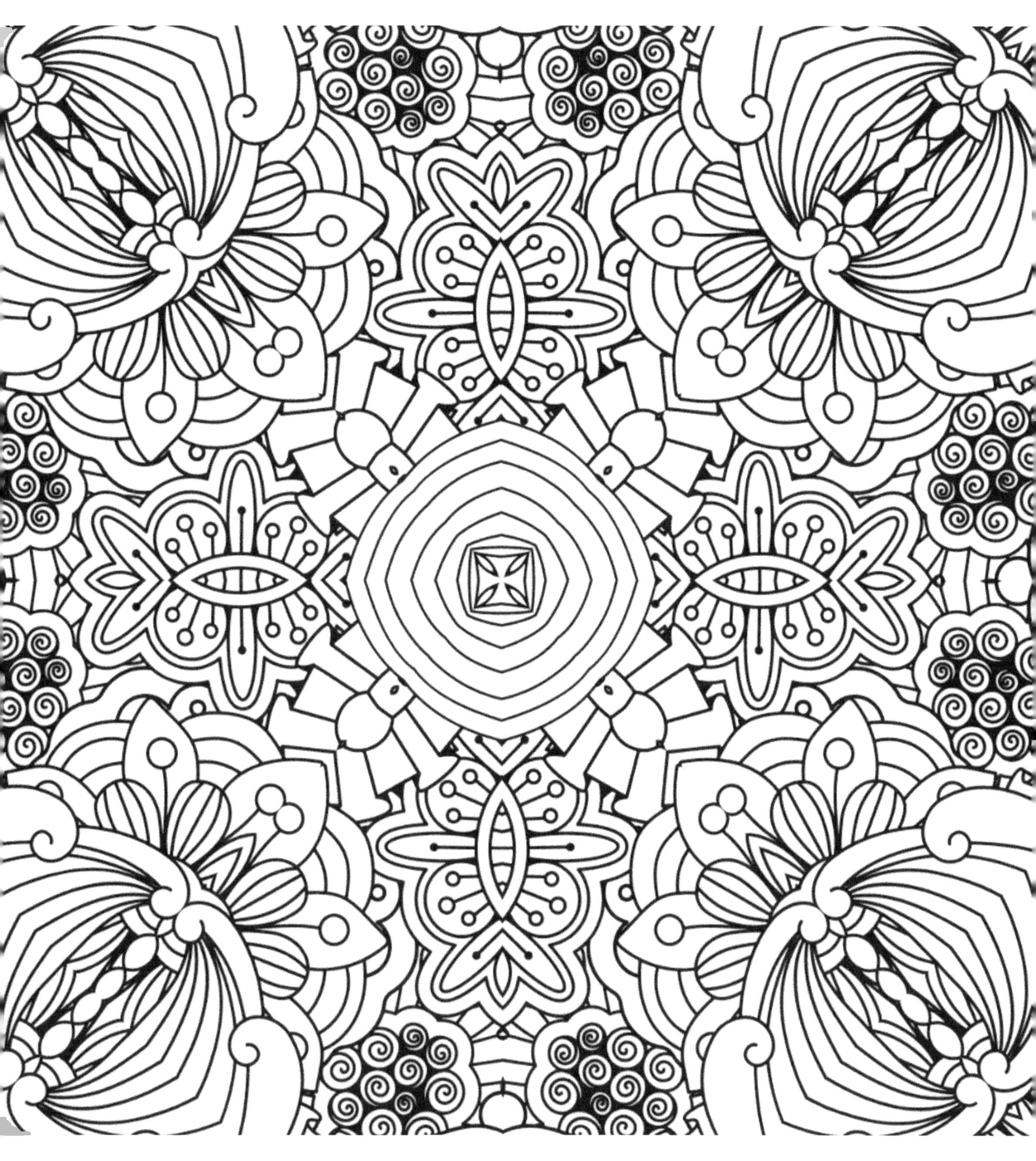